WUZZLES®

FOR PRESENTERS

STRETCHING EXERCISES FOR THE MIND

TOM UNDERWOOD

WITH AN INTRODUCTION BY BOB PIKE, CSP

Jossey-Bass
Pfeiffer

Published by

350 Sansome Street, 5th Floor
San Francisco, California 94104-1342
(415) 433-1740; Fax (415) 433-0499
(800) 274-4434; Fax (800) 569-0443

Visit our website at: www.pfeiffer.com

Cover design: *Brenda Duke*

Printing 10 9 8 7 6 5 4 3 2 1

This book is printed on acid-free, recycled stock that meets or exceeds the minimum GPO and EPA requirements for recycled paper.

TABLE OF CONTENTS

Introduction by Robert W. Pike

 to the wonderful world of WUZZLES®.

WUZZLES® are perfect as a way to involve people at any point in a presentation: as people are waiting for a session to start, for those that are back early from a break, or as an energizer to give people a mental break yet keep them focused.

These WUZZLES® contain added value from those that you may have seen in your newspaper. We've worked with WUZZLES® creator Tom Underwood to put together categories specific to many of the most common presentation topics including business/sales, communications, customer service, education, finance/banking, government, health care, legal, management, manufacturing, sports, technical, and much more!

One of the key ideas for getting the most out of a wuzzle is the setup. Most often people show a wuzzle and say "can you solve this?" Try being more creative and imaginative. Within each page of six, the WUZZLES® go from simple (the first one) to more complex (the last one). Try awarding yourself points per wuzzle, 1 for the easiest, 6 for the most difficult. Have small groups of 5–7 work together to solve them. Have each group explore how the meaning of the wuzzle applies to the presentation topic. Have people try to create their own to represent the presentation topic (you'd be surprised at some people's creativity!)

(As a matter of fact submit your best examples for possible inclusion in future editions.)

Each page is designed to be reproduced as a transparency so that you can project it for your audience. The WUZZLES® have been specially typeset to maximize their readability. So the next time you want to open, close, energize, reinforce, or change pace—reach for a wuzzle!

Wuzzles® for Presenters

Wuzzles® (or rebuses) are word puzzles made up of combinations of words, letters, figures or symbols that are positioned to create words, phrases, names, places, sayings, etc.

Some Wuzzles® contain more than one concept and some can be created in several different ways. For example, here are four of the many versions of "SPLIT UP OVER NOTHING".

$\dfrac{\text{SPLIT}}{\text{NOTHING}}$	$\dfrac{\text{U} \qquad \text{P}}{\text{NOTHING}}$	$\dfrac{\text{SPLIT UP}}{\text{O}}$	T I L P S

Some Wuzzles® can contain as many as six concepts such as:

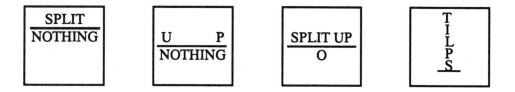

(A little misunderstanding between a couple of close friends.)

Or one word can create twelve different WUZZLES® and twelve different concepts such as the word "ALL".

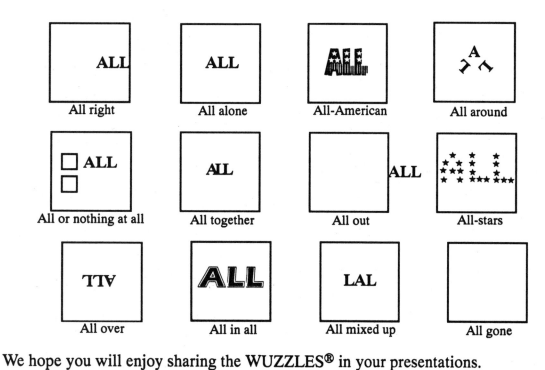

We hope you will enjoy sharing the WUZZLES® in your presentations.

We as publishers would like to acknowledge the following individuals: Doug McCallum, Rebecca Tolle, and Sandi Dufault. Without their support, time, patience and enthusiasm this project would never have been made possible.

Business/Sales

DEAL

Answer: A big deal

Business/Sales

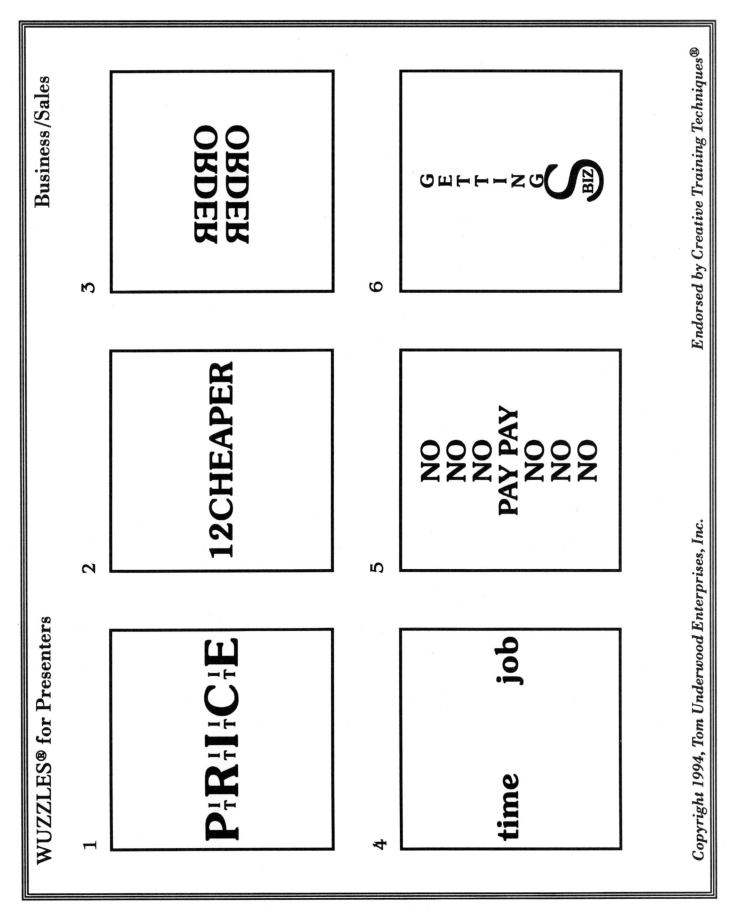

1

2

3

4

5

6

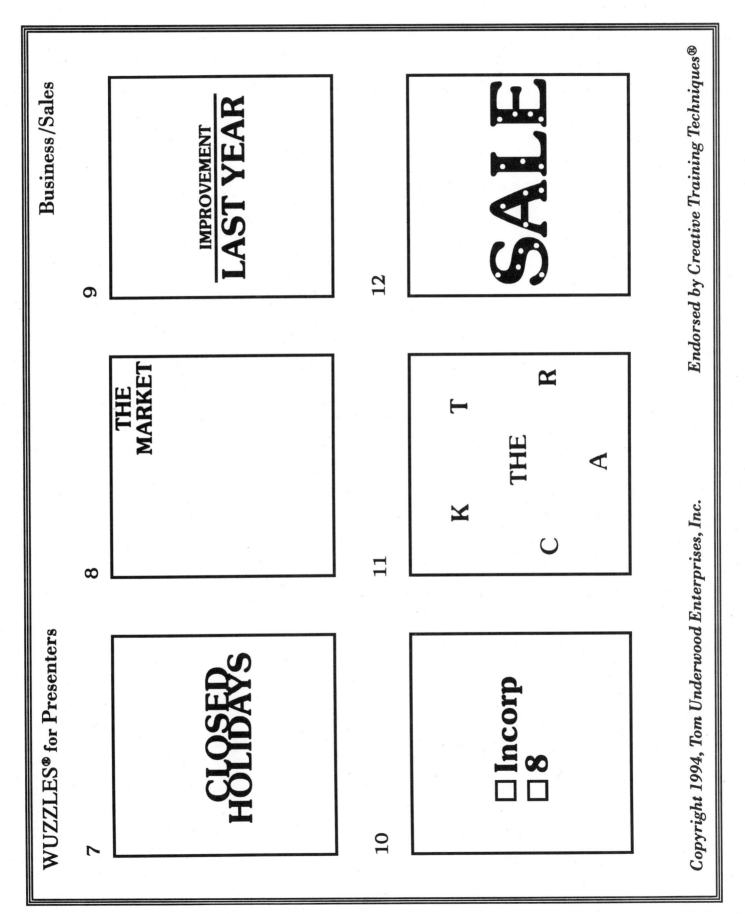

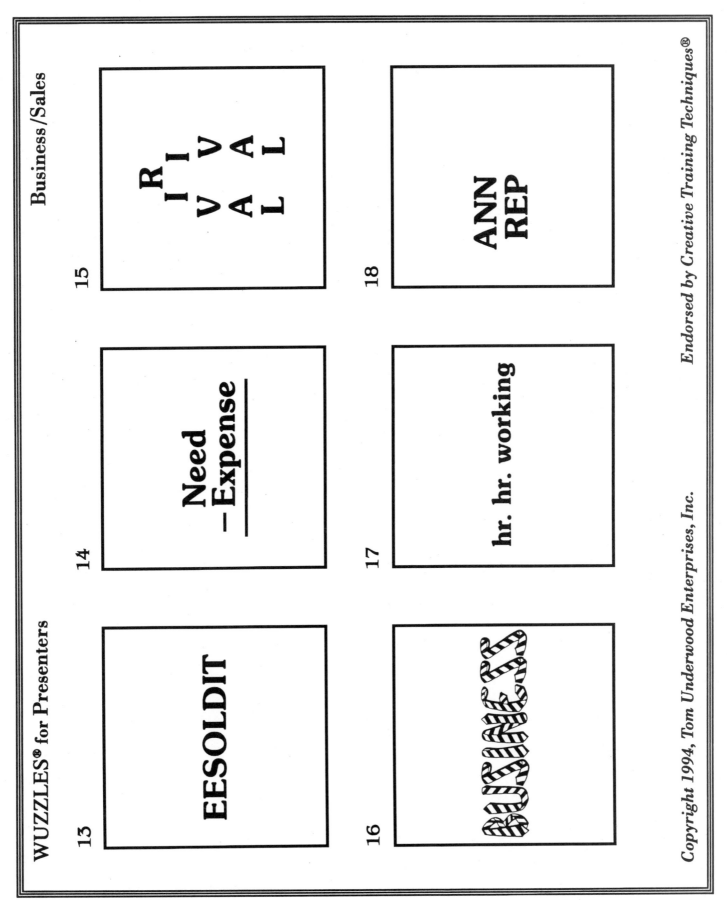

13 EESOLDIT

14
Need
–Expense
———

15
R
I I
V V
A A
L L

16 BUSINESS

17 hr. hr. working

18 ANN
REP

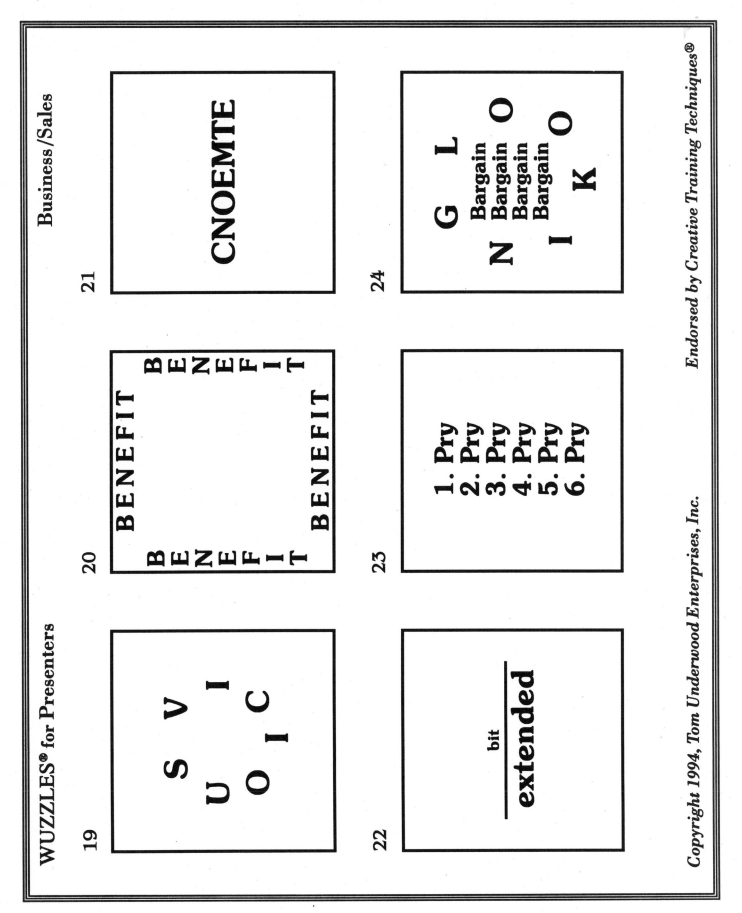

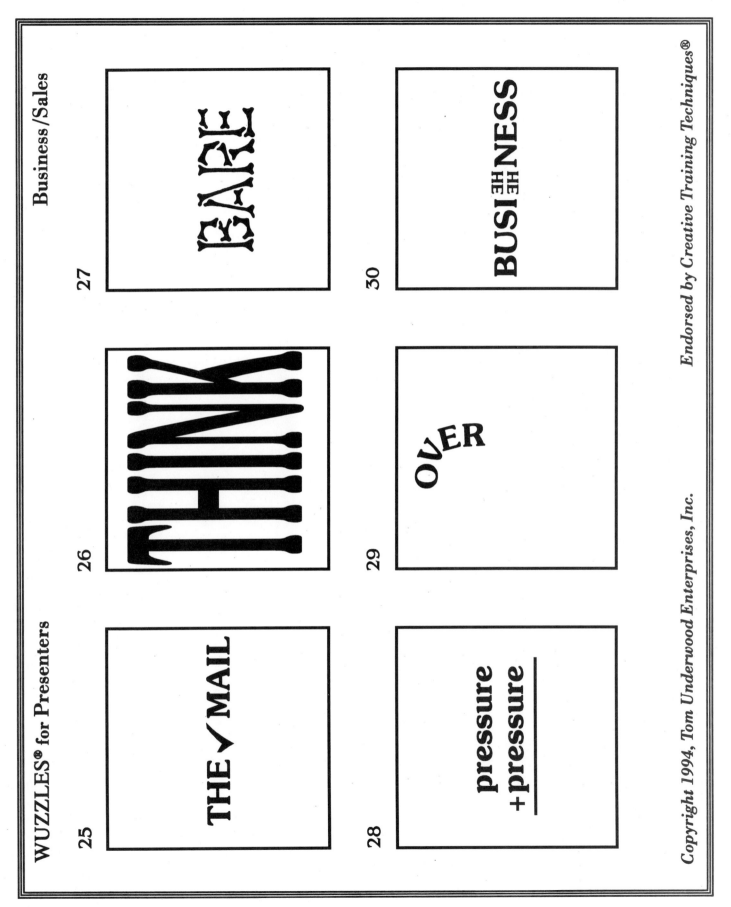

25

THE ✓ MAIL

26

THINK

27

BARE

28

pressure
+pressure

29

OVER

30

BUSI ᴛʜᴇ ᴛʜᴇ NESS

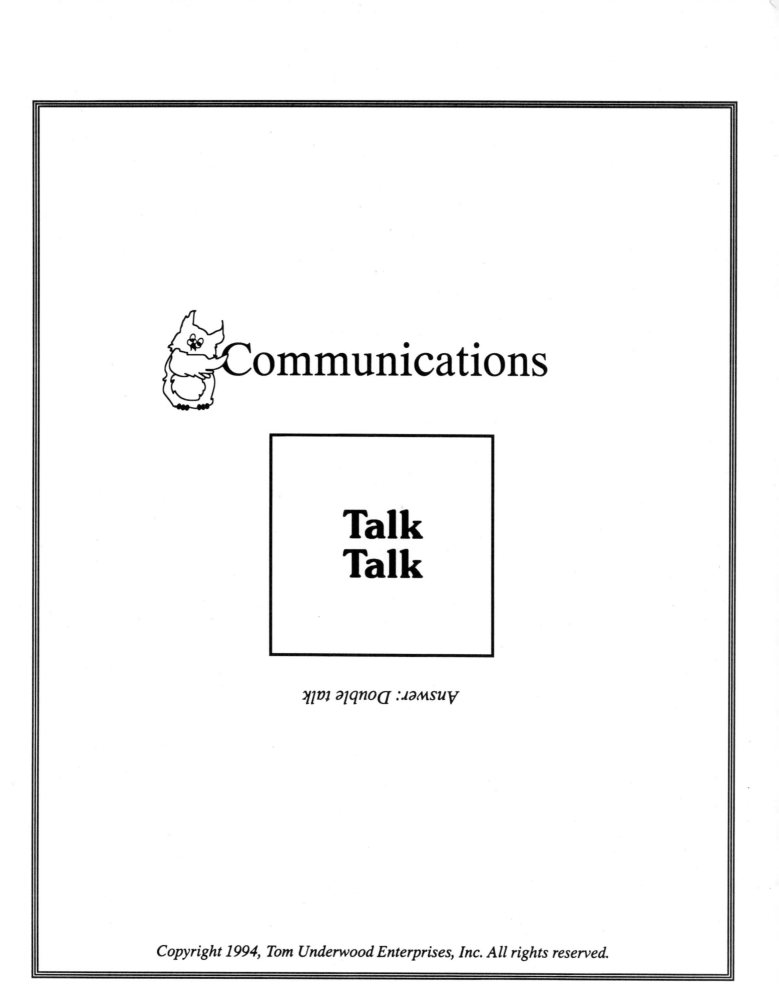Communications

**Talk
Talk**

Answer: Double talk

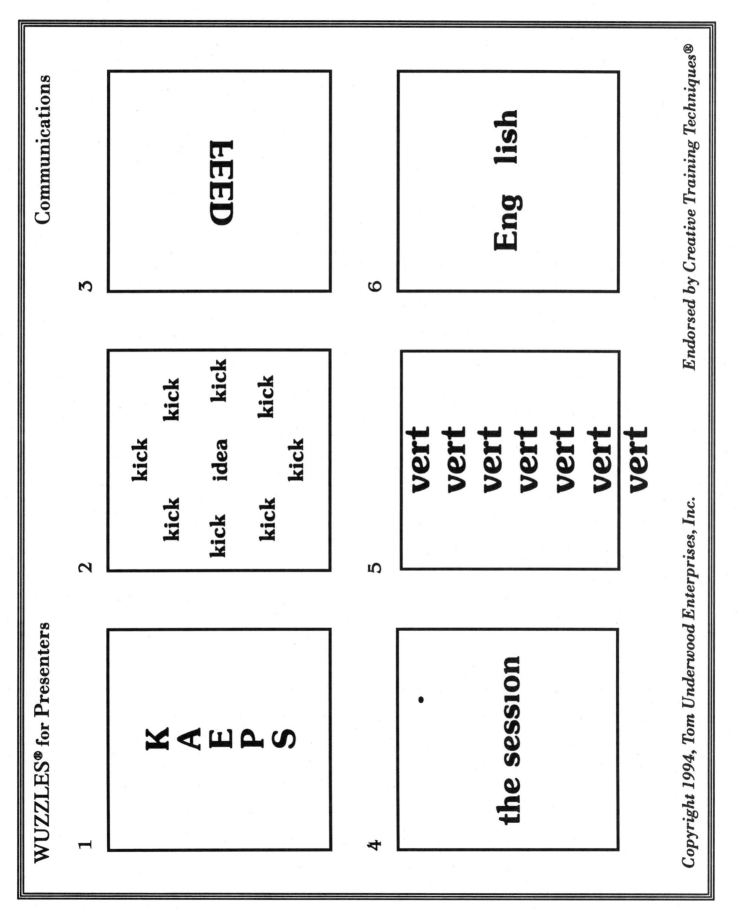

1

K
A
E
P
S

2

kick   kick

kick

kick   idea   kick

kick   kick

kick

3

ⅎEED

4

.

the session

5

vert
vert
vert
vert
vert
vert
vert

6

Eng   lish

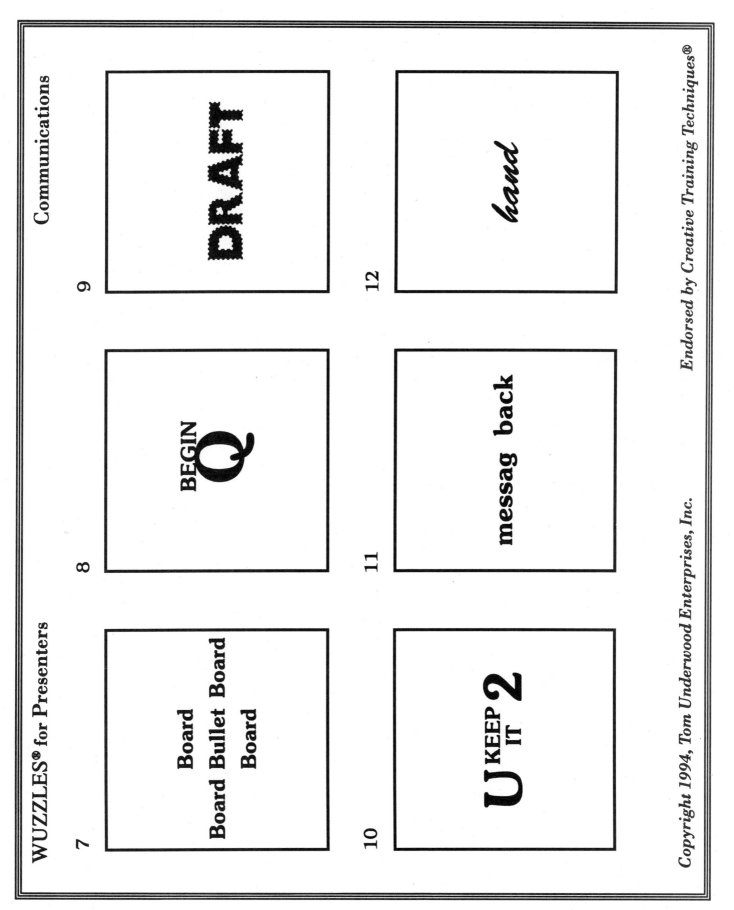

7

Board
Board Bullet Board
Board

8

BEGIN
Q

9

DRAFT

10

U KEEP IT 2

11

messag back

12

hand

Endorsed by Creative Training Techniques®

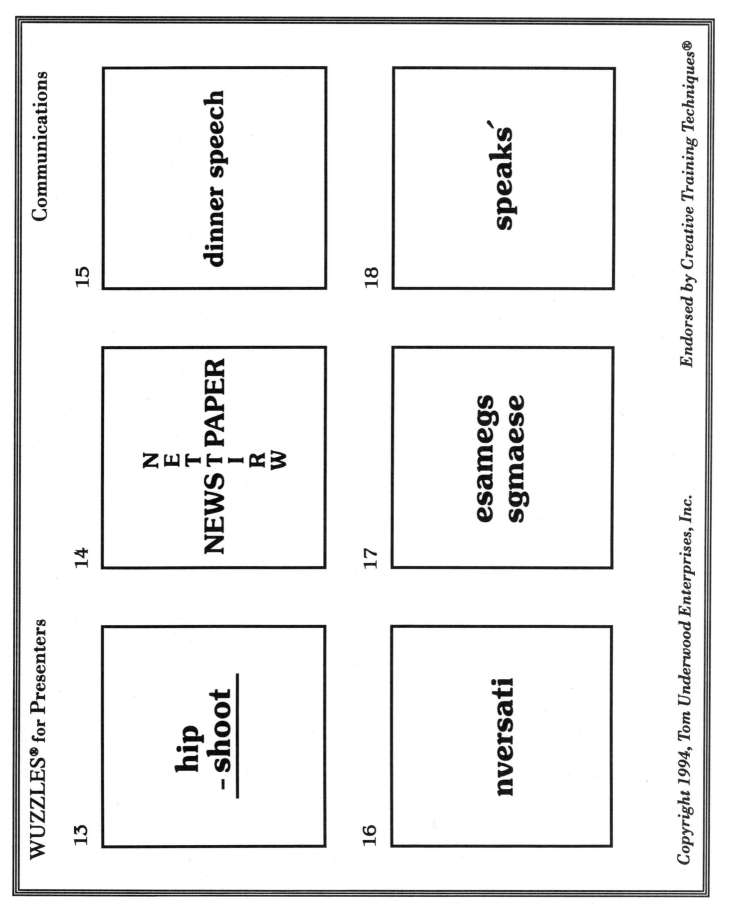

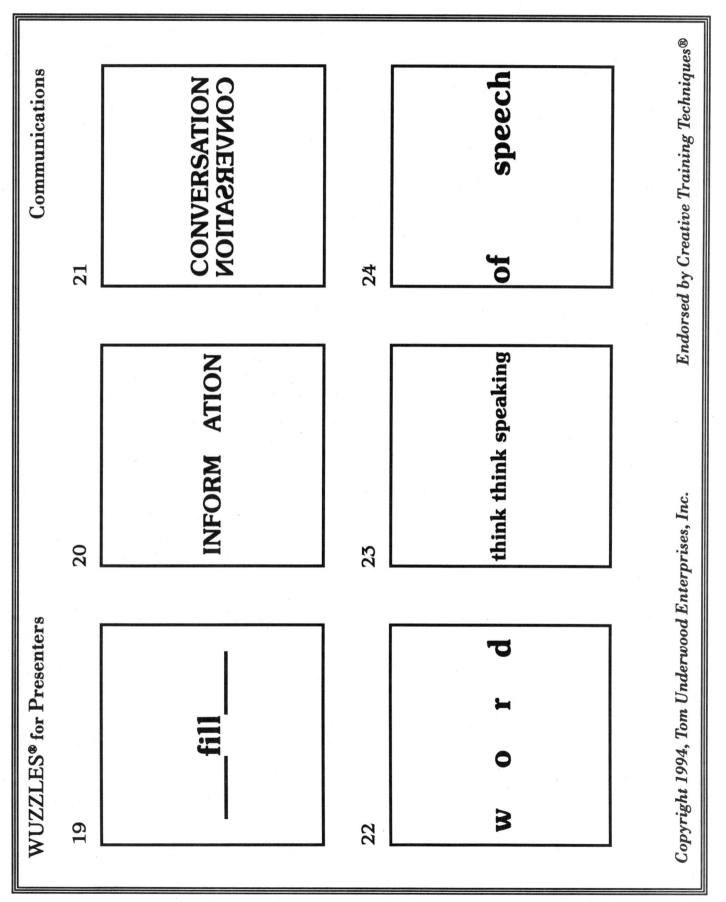

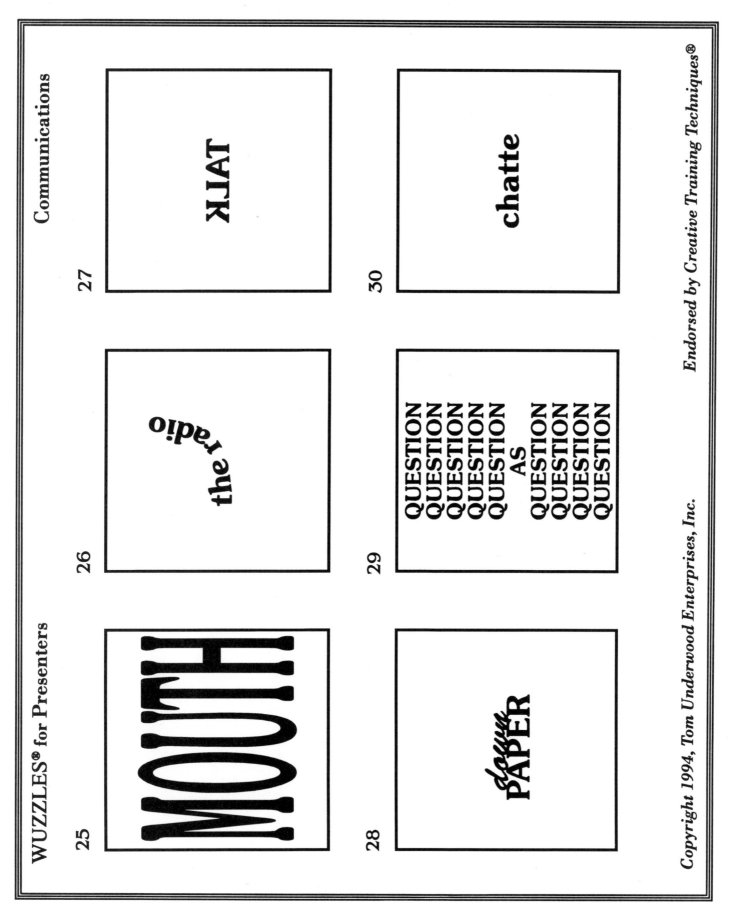

WUZZLES® for Presenters

Communications

25 — MOUTH (stretched)

26 — the radio (upside down)

27 — TALK (upside down)

28 — slurm PAPER

29 — QUESTION QUESTION QUESTION QUESTION QUESTION AS QUESTION QUESTION QUESTION QUESTION QUESTION

30 — chatte

Endorsed by Creative Training Techniques®

Customer Service

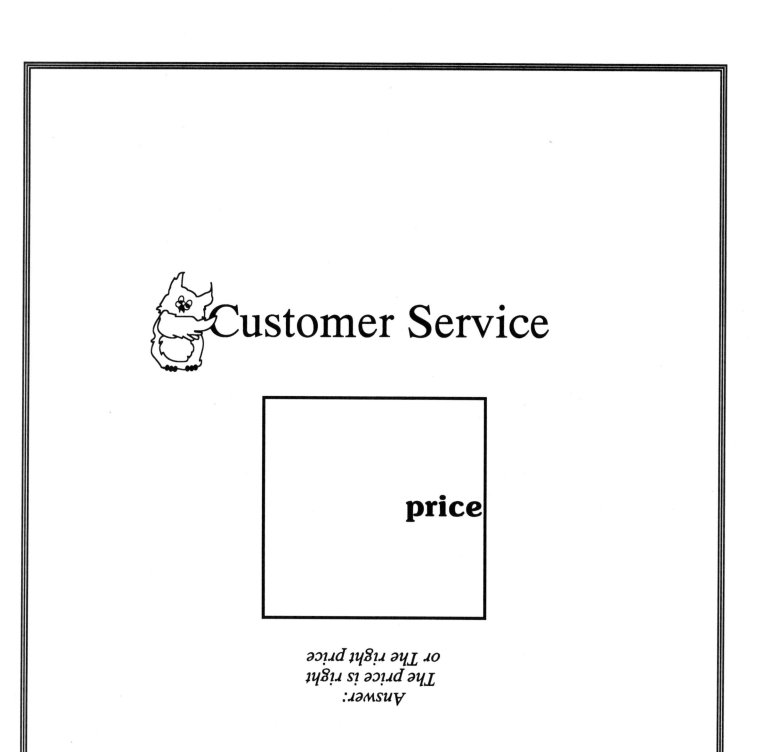

price

Answer:
The price is right
or The right price

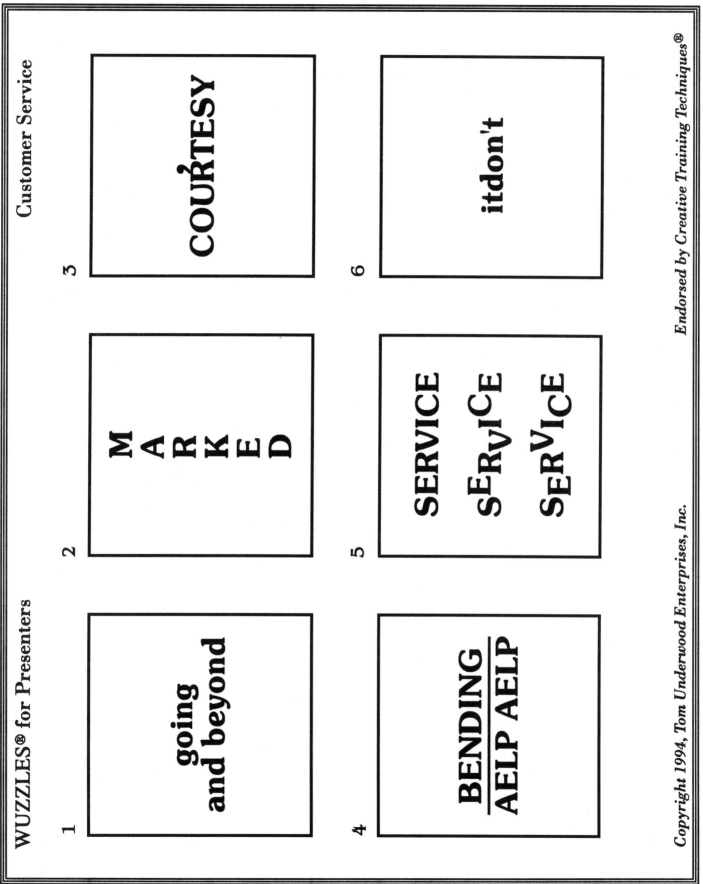

Customer Service

1

going
and beyond

2

M
A
R
K
E
D

3

COURTESY

4

BENDING
—————
AELP AELP

5

SERVICE
sERvICE
sERVIcE

6

itdon't

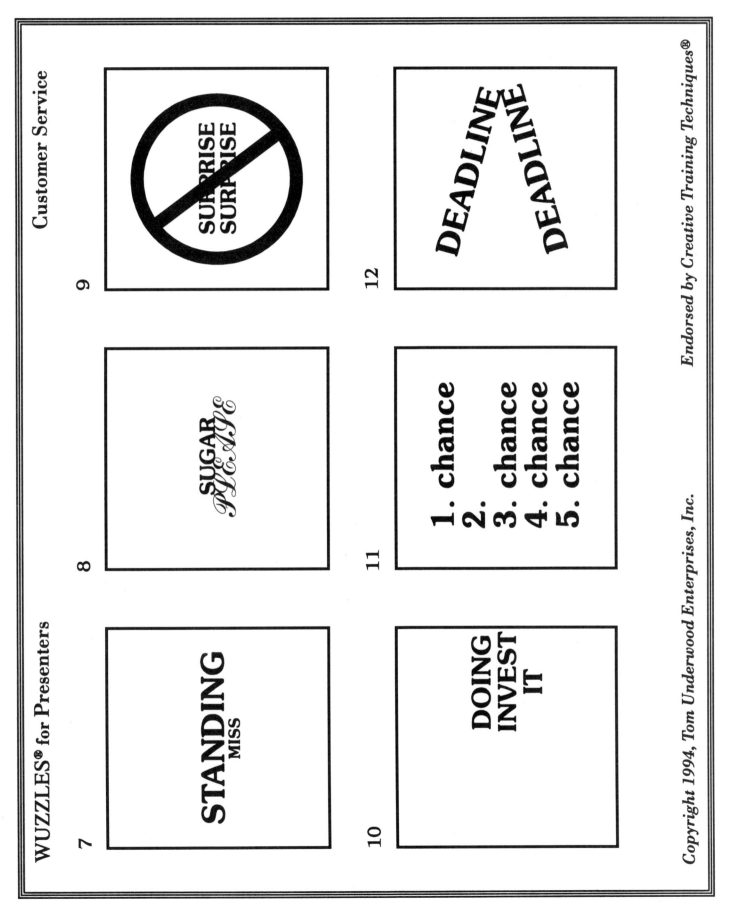

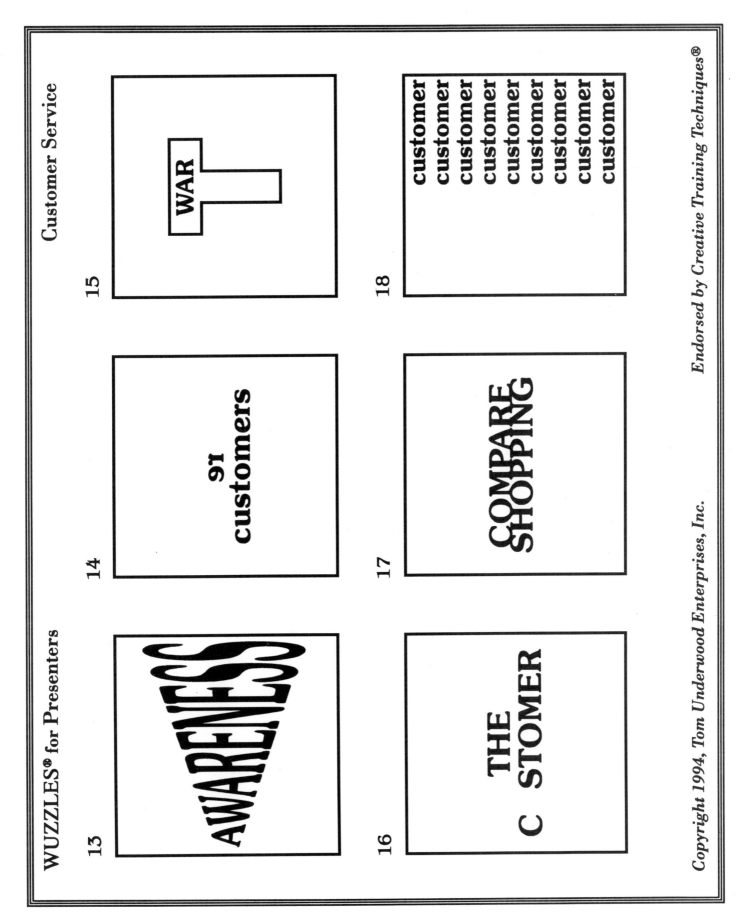

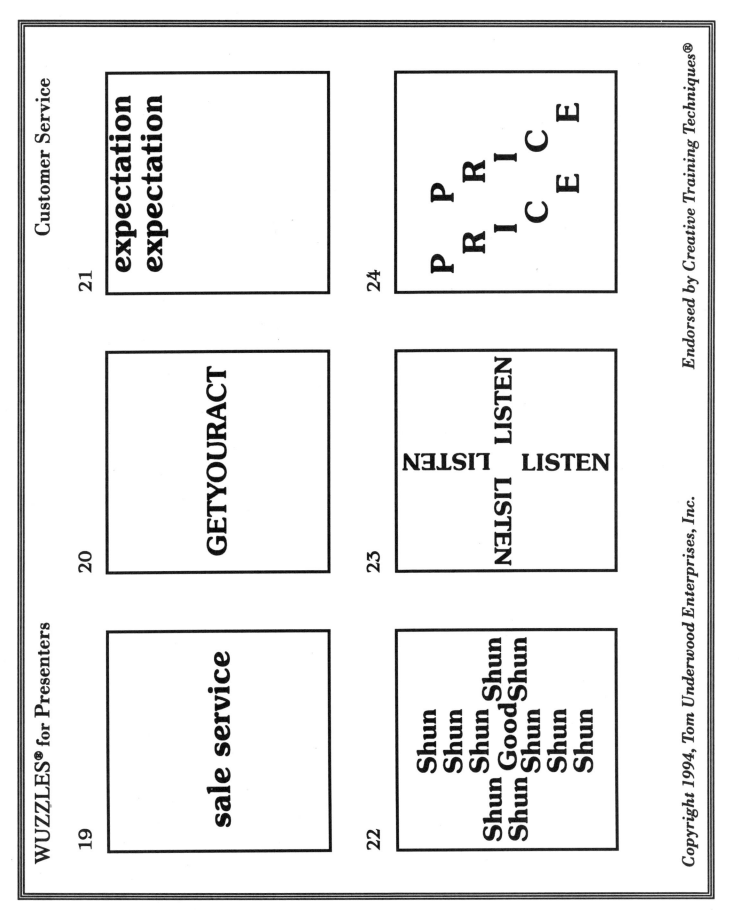

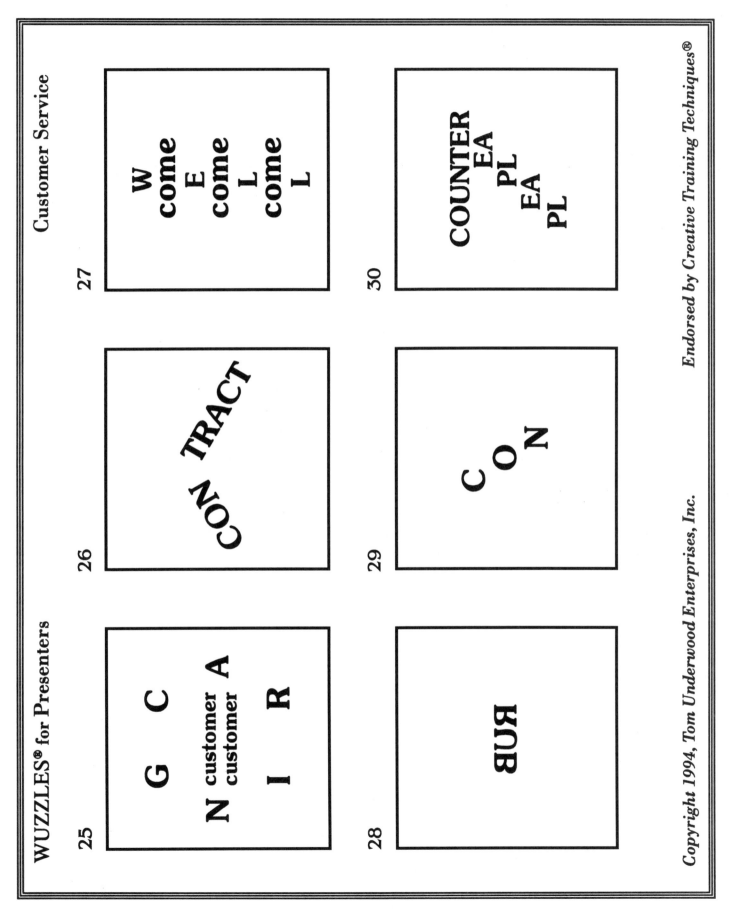

25

G   C

N customer A
customer

I   R

26

CON TRACT

27

W
  come
  E
    come
    L
      come
      L

28

ЯUB

29

C   O
      N

30

COUNTER
EA
PL
EA
PL

Endorsed by Creative Training Techniques®

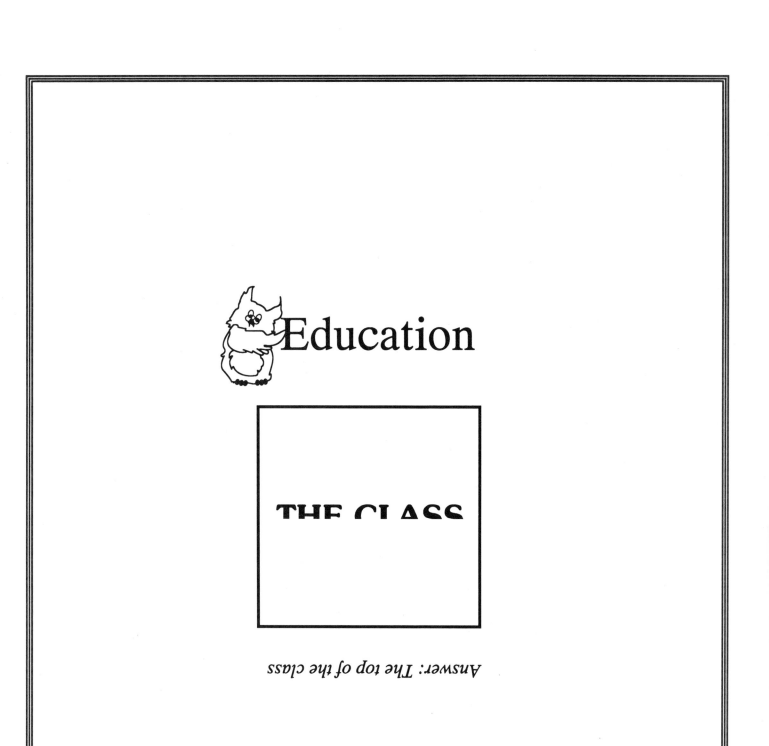

Education

THE CLASS

Answer: The top of the class

Education

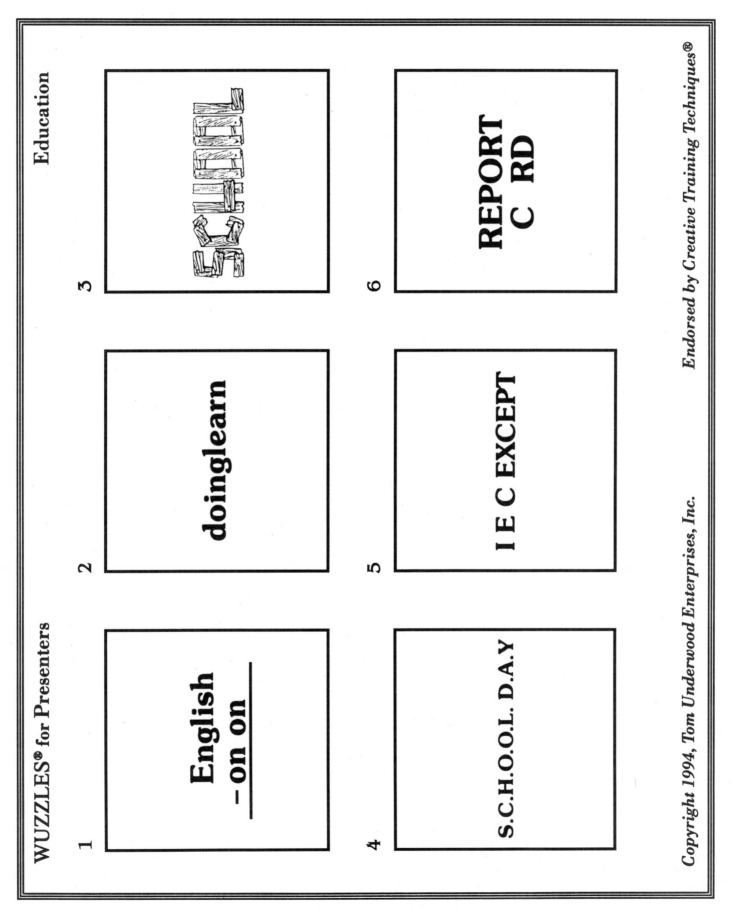

1

English
– on on

2

doinglearn

3

4

S.C.H.O.O.L. D.A.Y

5

I E C EXCEPT

6

REPORT
C RD

Education

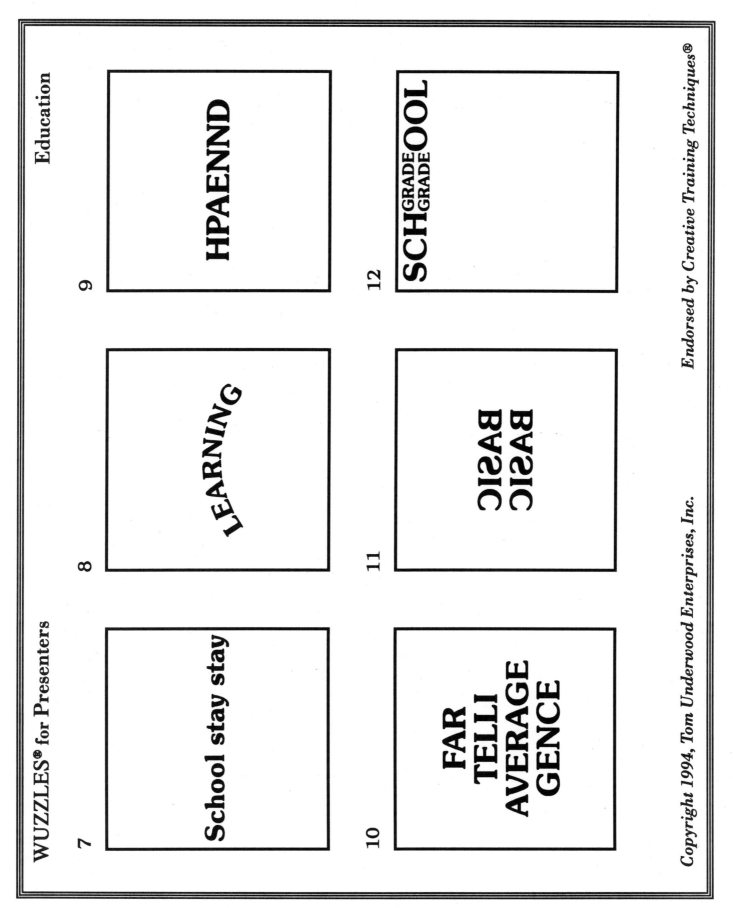

Endorsed by Creative Training Techniques®

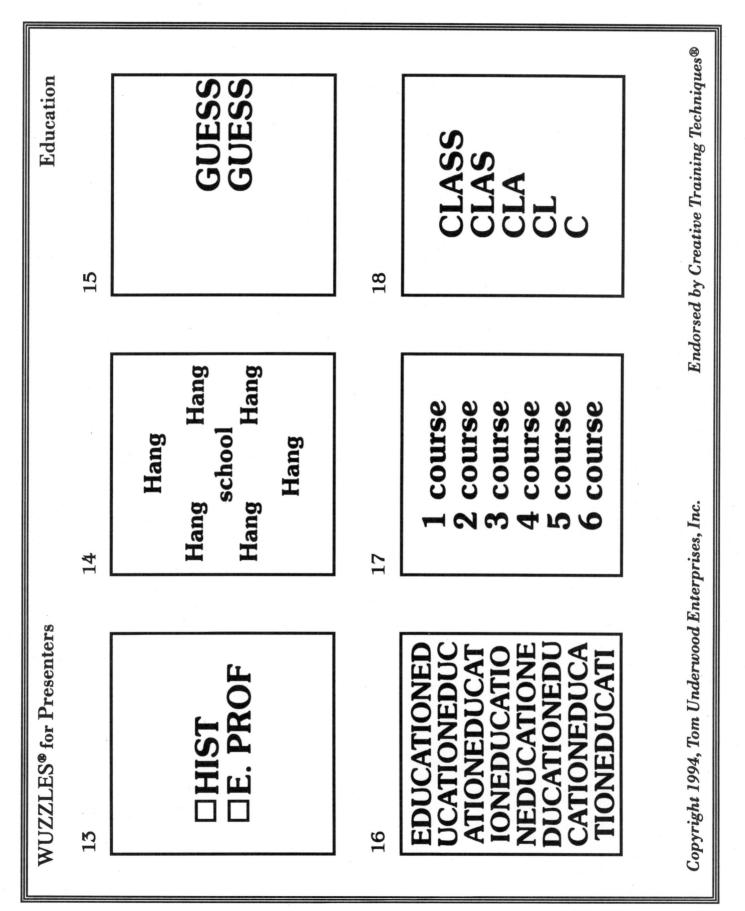

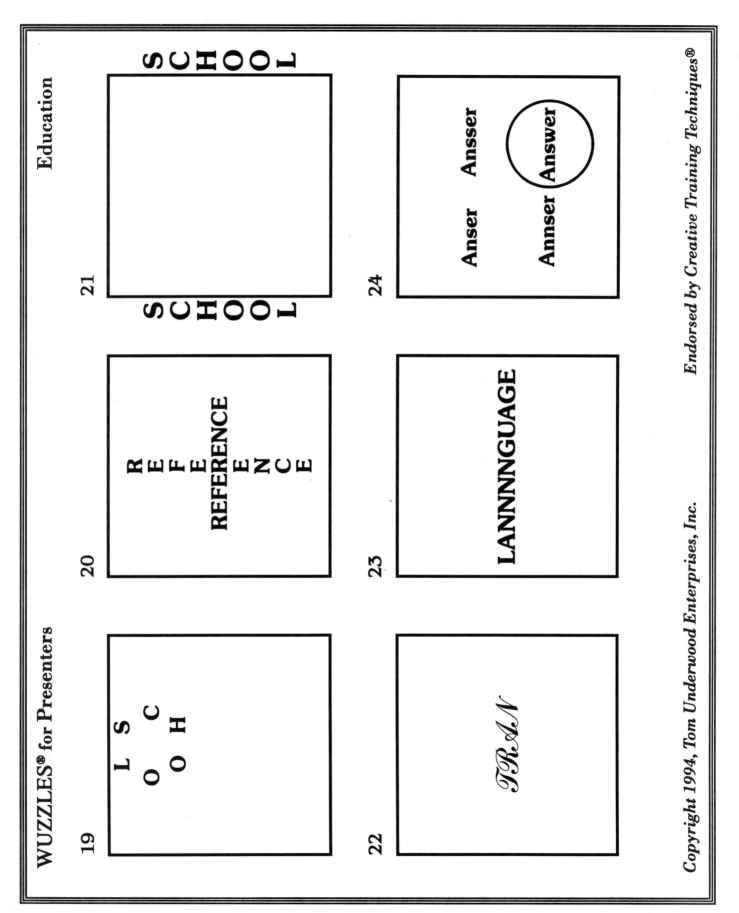

WUZZLES® for Presenters   Education

19
```
   L   S
 O   C
   O   H
```

20
```
    R
    E
    F
    E
REFERENCE
    E
    N
    C
    E
```

21
```
S         S
C         C
H         H
O         O
O         O
L         L
```

22

TRAN

23

LANNNNGUAGE

24

Anser   Ansser

Anser

Annser   (Answer)

Education

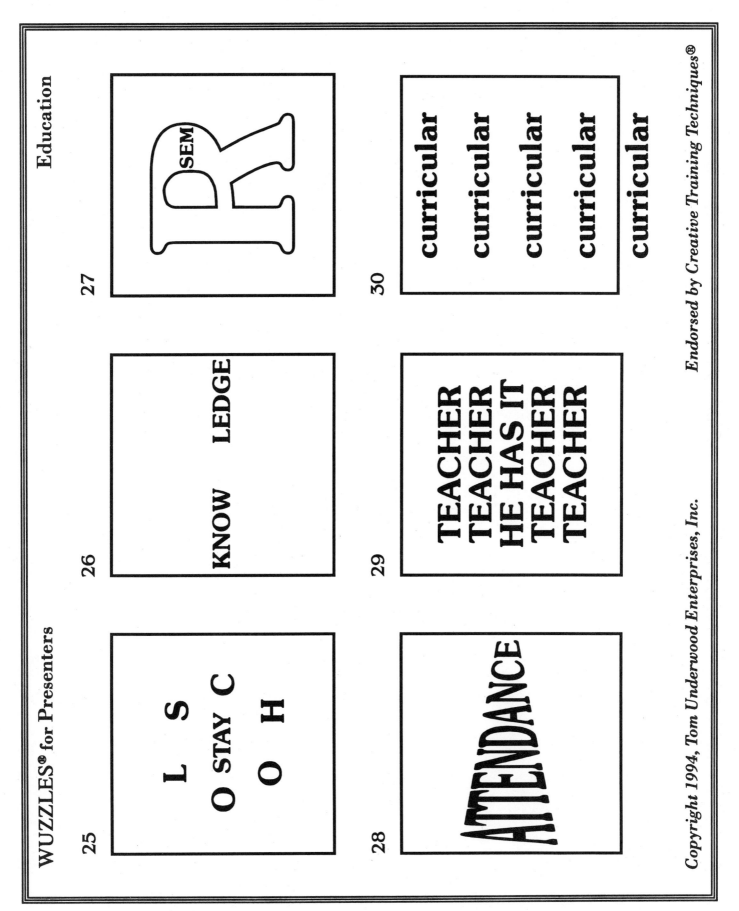

25

L   S
O STAY C
O   H

26

KNOW   LEDGE

27

R
SEM

28

ATTENDANCE

29

TEACHER
TEACHER
HE HAS IT
TEACHER
TEACHER

30

curricular
curricular
curricular
curricular
curricular

Finance/Banking

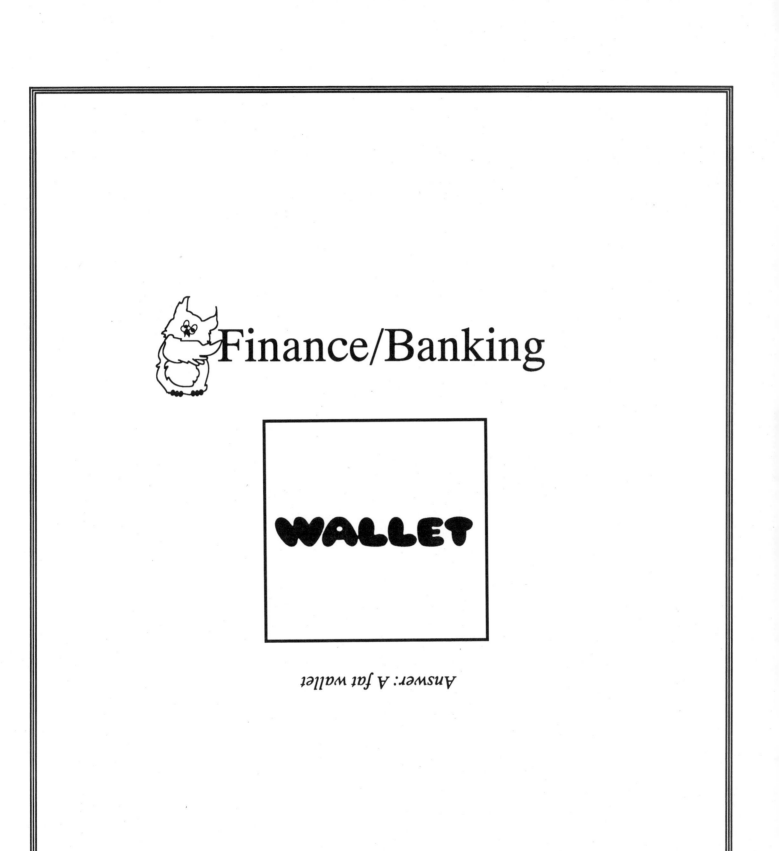

Answer: A fat wallet

Finance/Banking

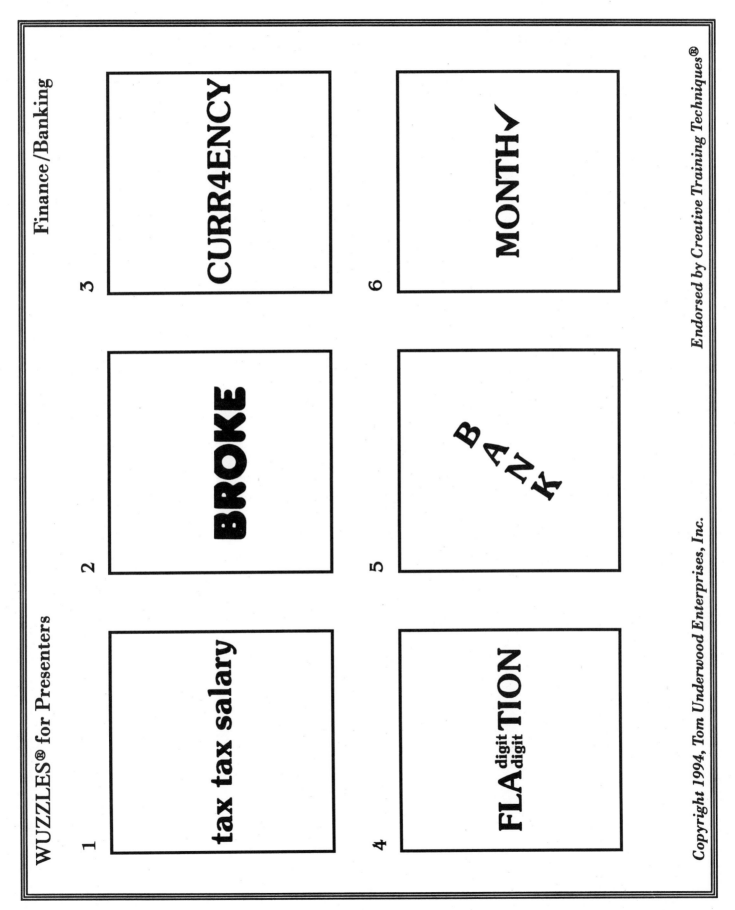

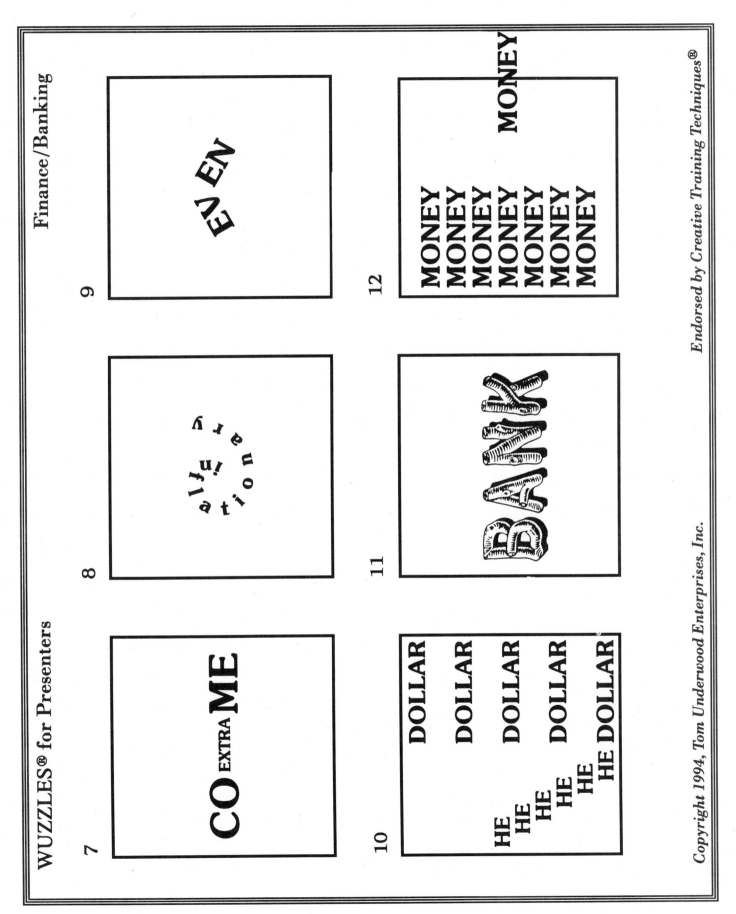

7. CO EXTRA **ME**

8. inflationary

9. EV EN

10. DOLLAR DOLLAR DOLLAR DOLLAR HE DOLLAR HE HE HE HE

11. BANK

12. MONEY MONEY MONEY MONEY MONEY MONEY MONEY MONEY

Finance/Banking

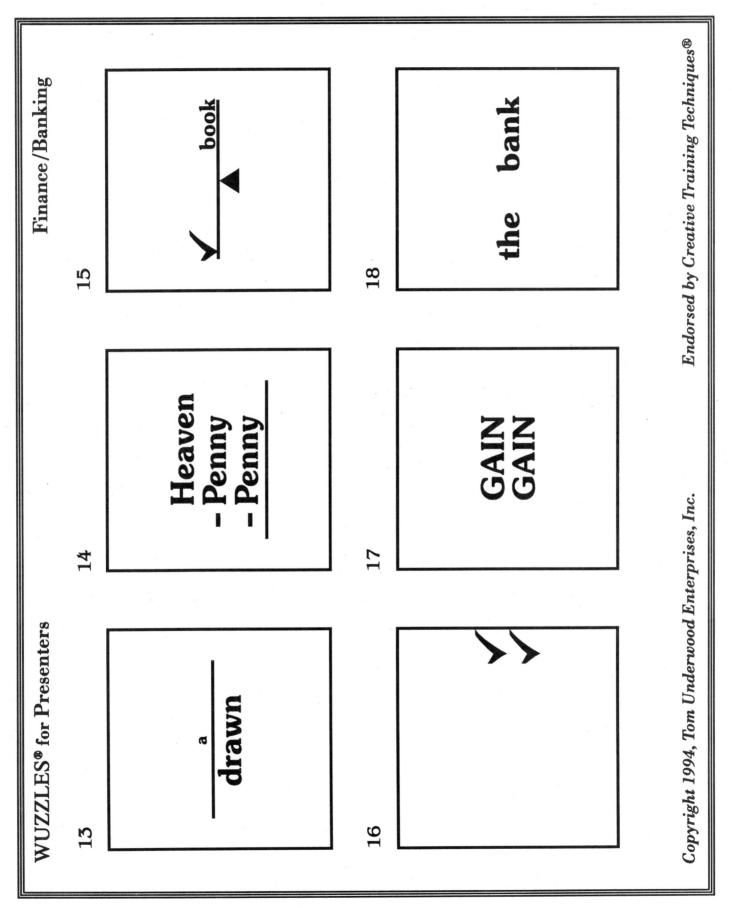

13

a
_____
drawn

14

Heaven
- Penny
- Penny
_____

15

book
▲

16

》》

17

GAIN
GAIN

18

the   bank

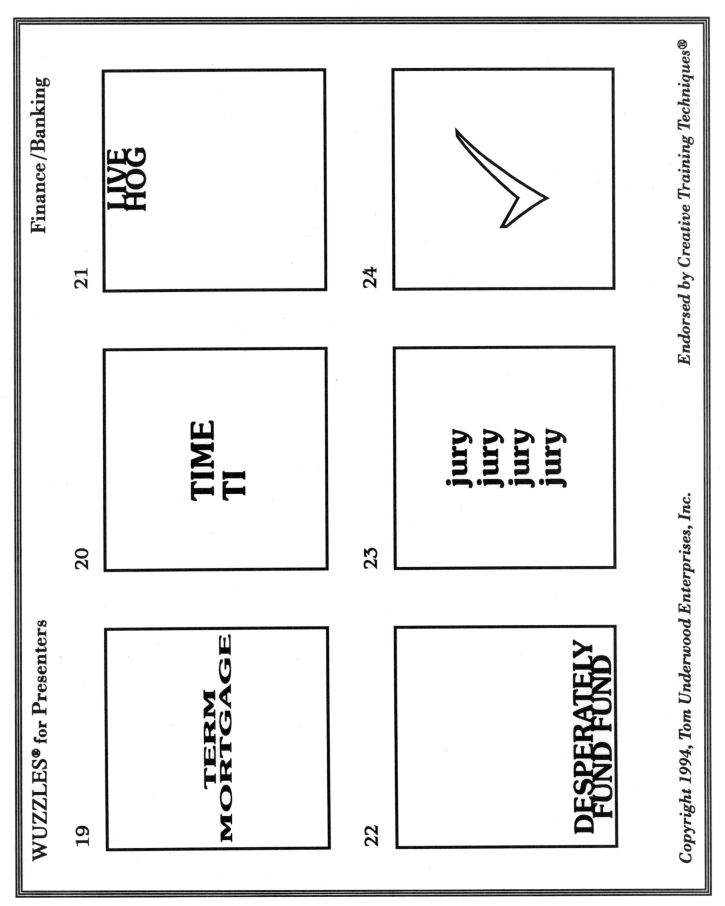

19

TERM
MORTGAGE

20

TIME
TI

21

LIVE
HOG

22

DESPERATELY
FUND FUND

23

jury
jury
jury
jury

24

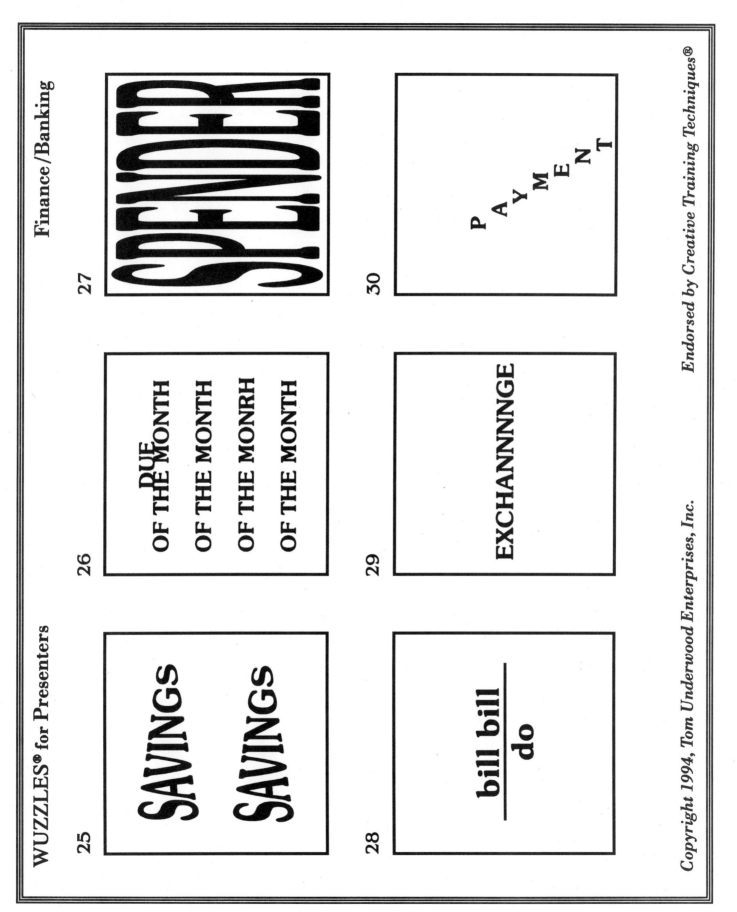

25 SAVINGS SAVINGS

26 DUE OF THE MONTH OF THE MONTH OF THE MONRH OF THE MONTH

27 SPENDER

28 bill bill / do

29 EXCHANNNNGE

30 P A Y M E N T

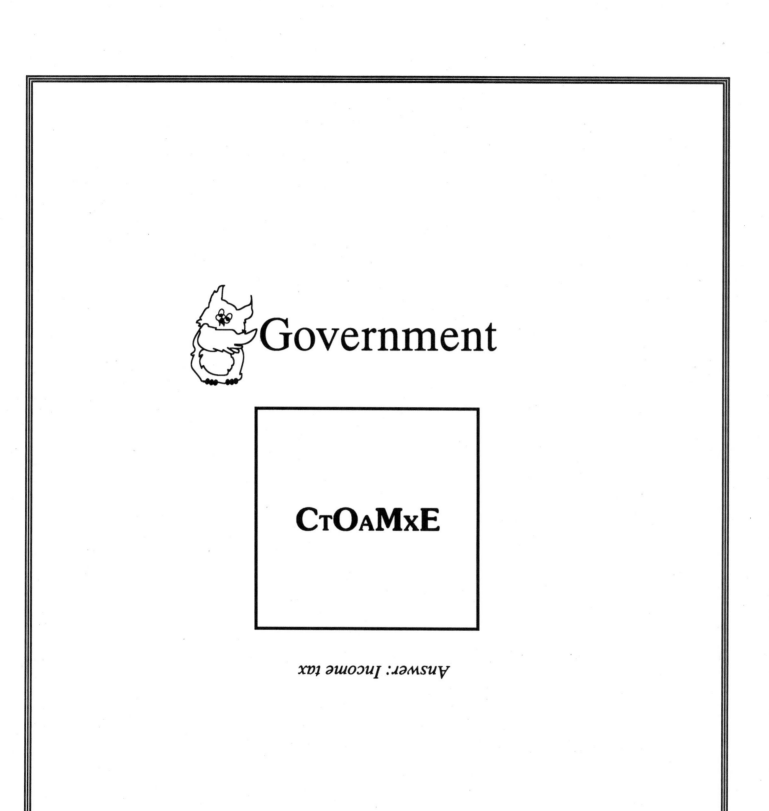

Government

CₜOₐMₓE

Answer: Income tax

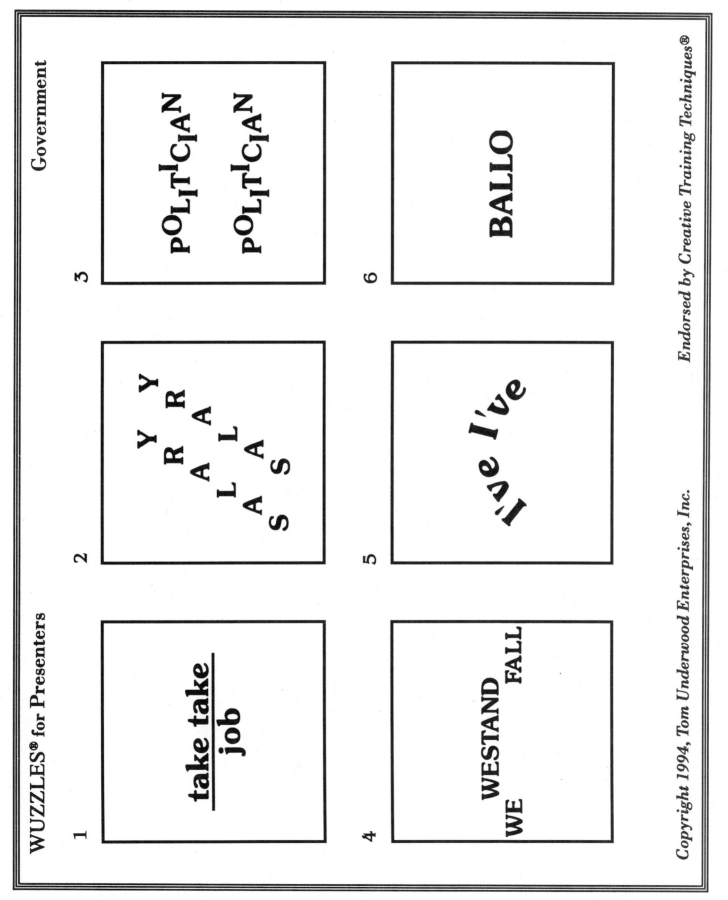

Government

1

take take
job

2

Y Y
R R
A A
L L
A A
S S

3

pO_LI_TI_CI_AN
pO_LI_TI_CI_AN

4

WESTAND
WE   FALL

5

I've I've

6

BALLO

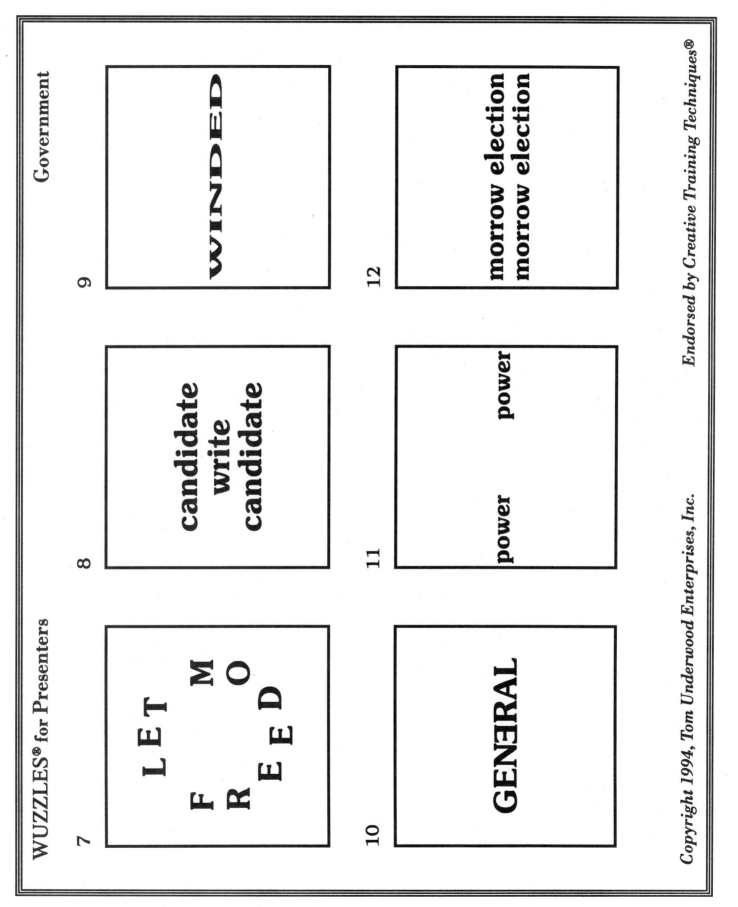

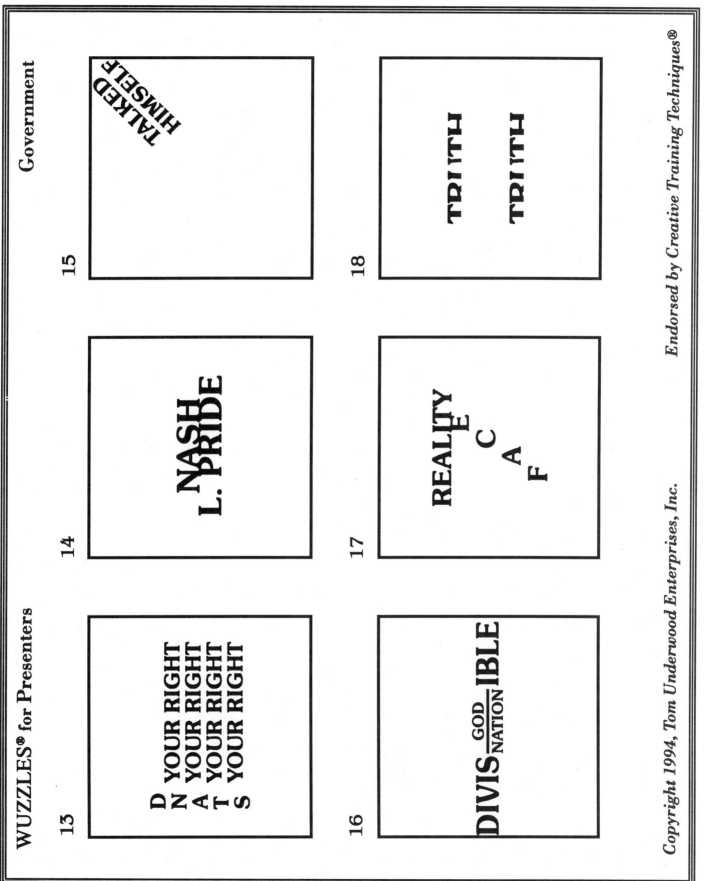

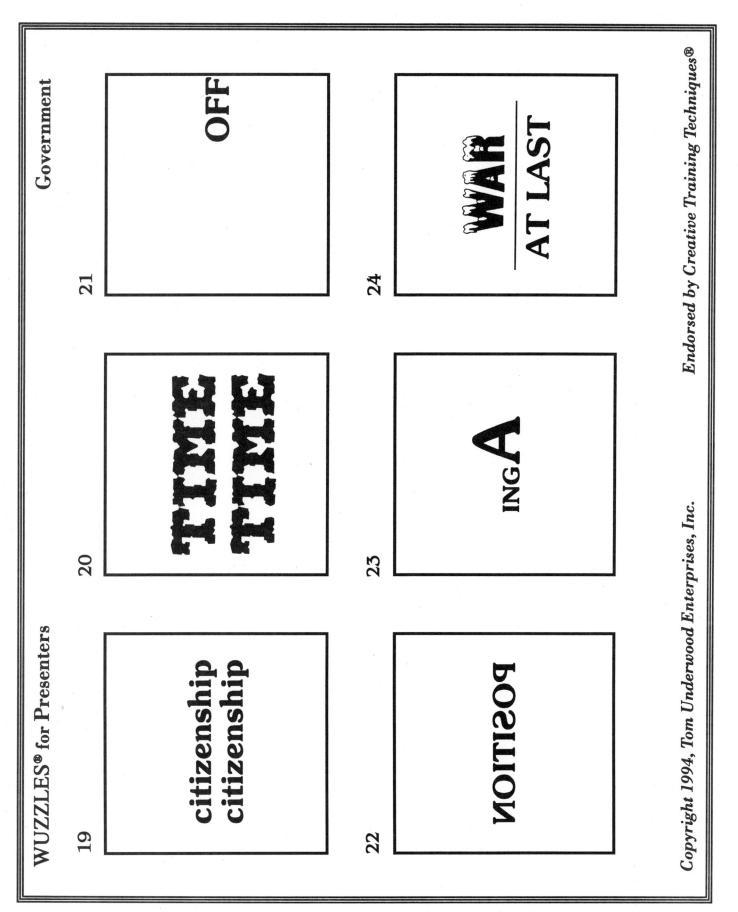

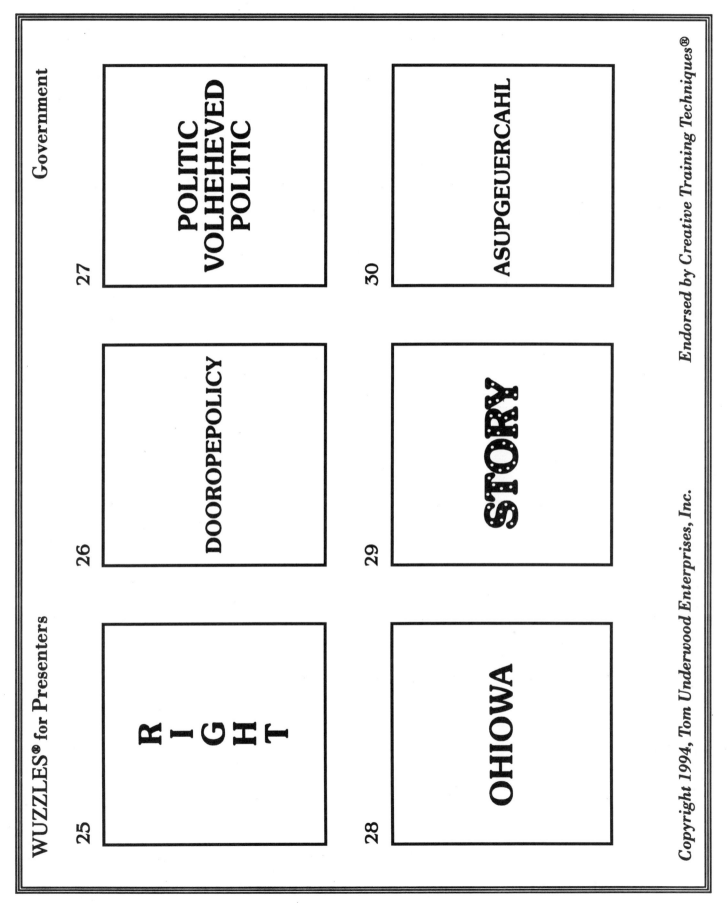

25

R
I
G
H
T

26

DOOROPEPOLICY

27

POLITIC
VOLHEHEVED
POLITIC

28

OHIOWA

29

STORY

30

ASUPGEUERCAHL

Health Care

COUGH

Answer: Cough drops

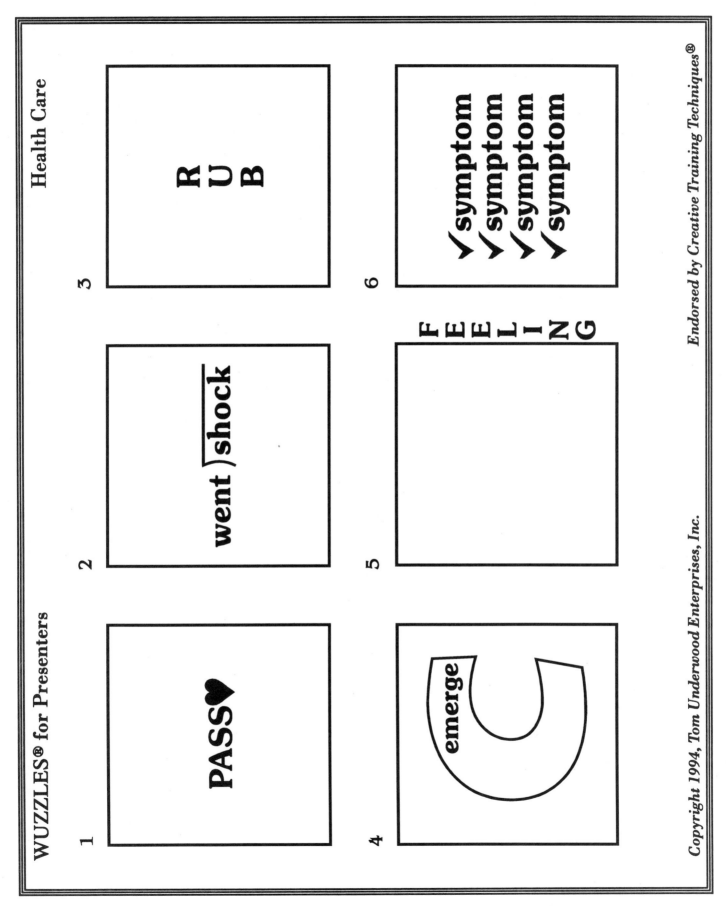

1

PASS♥

2

went)shock

3

R
U
B

4

emerge

5

F
E
E
L
I
N
G

6

✓symptom
✓symptom
✓symptom
✓symptom

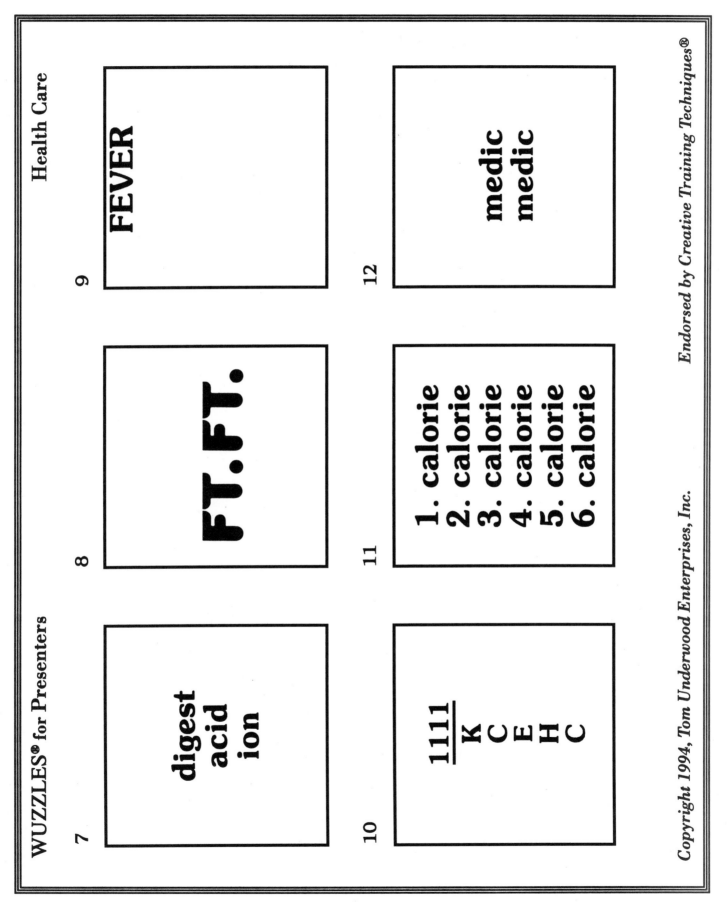

7

digest
acid
ion

8

FT.FT.

9

FEVER

10

$\dfrac{1111}{\begin{array}{c}K\\C\\E\\H\\C\end{array}}$

11

1. calorie
2. calorie
3. calorie
4. calorie
5. calorie
6. calorie

12

medic
medic

Health Care

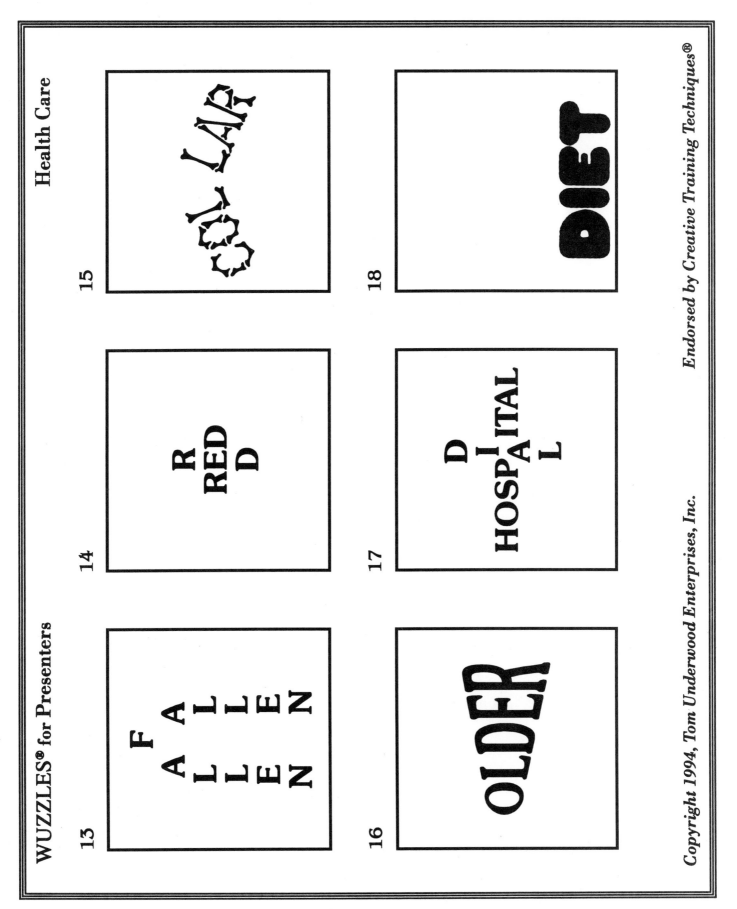

13

F
A A
L L
L L
E E
N N

14

R
RED
D

15

COLLAR

16

OLDER

17

D
I
HOSPAITAL
L

18

DIET

Health Care

19

DOUBLED
IN PAIN

20

COM
COLD

21

C
O
M PNEUMONIA
I
N
G

22

JURY
PAINFUL
JURY

23

F
E
E
DUMP L DUMP
I
N
G

24

FEC
LAIRET
TION

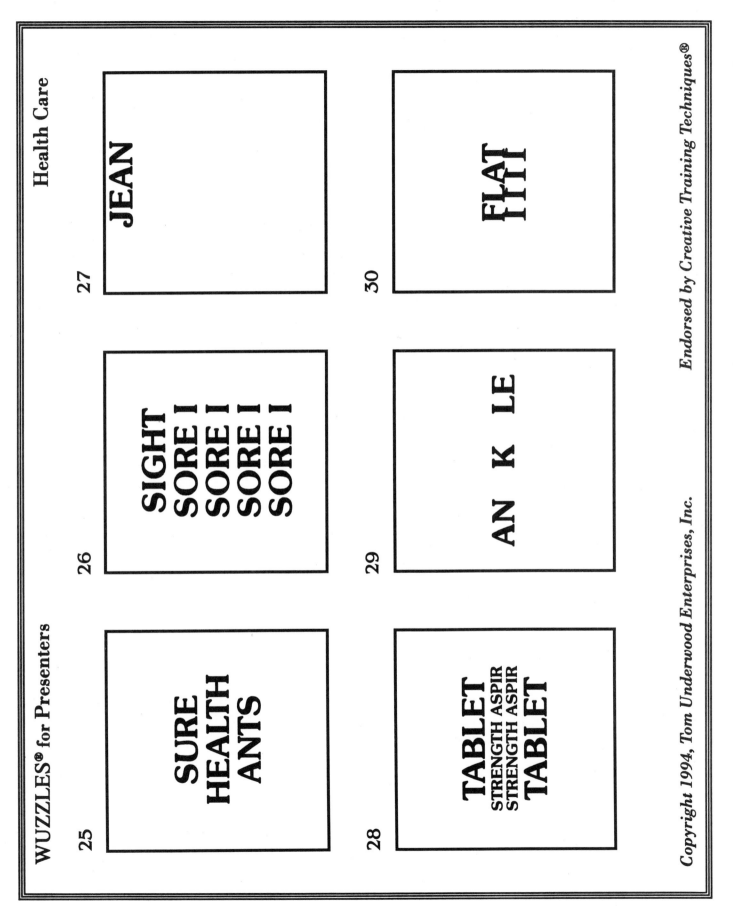

25 SURE
HEALTH
ANTS

26 SIGHT
SORE I
SORE I
SORE I
SORE I

27 JEAN

28 TABLET
STRENGTH ASPIR
STRENGTH ASPIR
TABLET

29 AN K LE

30 FLAT

Legal

Bad
+Vice

Answer: Bad advice

Legal

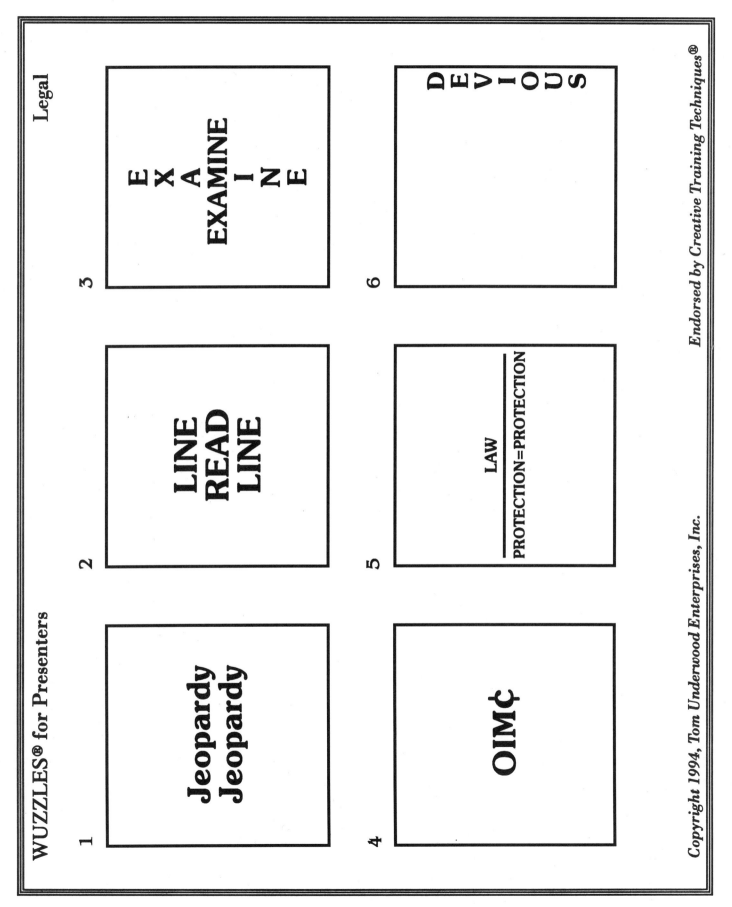

1

Jeopardy
Jeopardy

2

LINE
READ
LINE

3

E
X
A
EXAMINE
I
N
E

4

OIM¢

5

LAW

PROTECTION=PROTECTION

6

D
E
V
I
O
S

Copyright 1994, Tom Underwood Enterprises, Inc.

Endorsed by Creative Training Techniques®

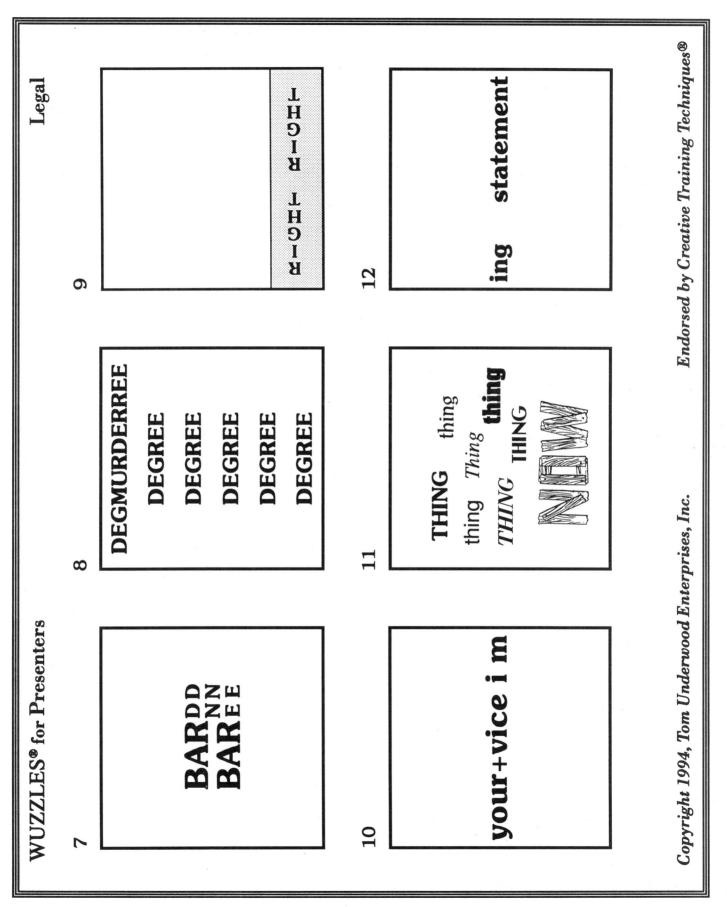

7

BARDD
NN
BAREE

8

DEGMURDERREE

DEGREE

DEGREE

DEGREE

DEGREE

DEGREE

9

RIGHT RIGHT

10

your+vice i m

11

THING thing
thing *Thing* **thing**
thing *THING* THING
NEW

12

ing   statement

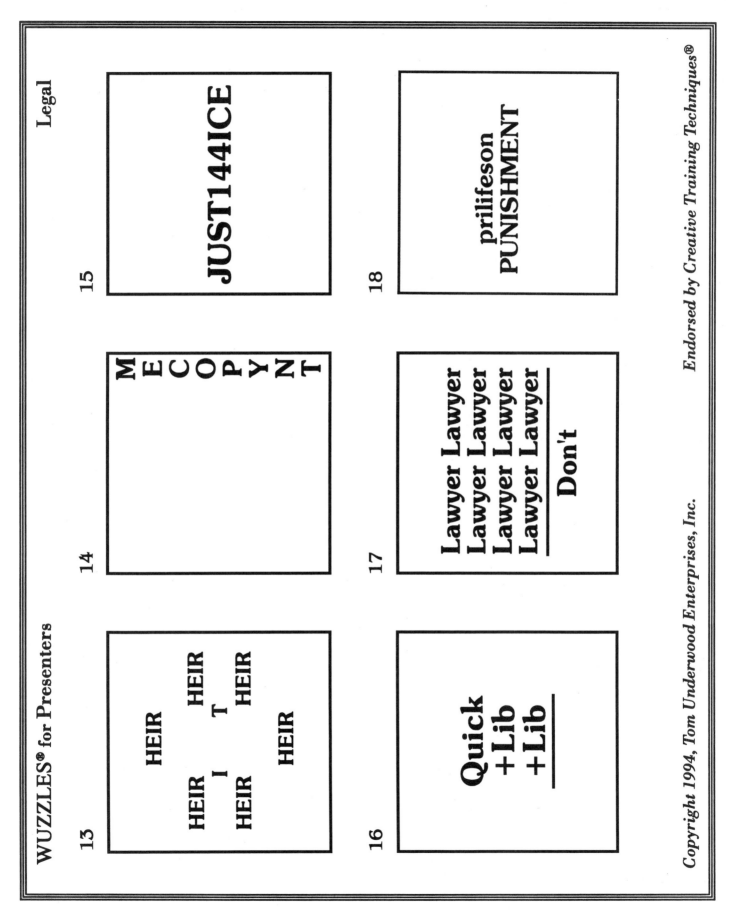

13

HEIR   HEIR
HEIR   I   T   HEIR
HEIR   HEIR

14

M
E
C
O
P
Y
N
T

15

JUST144ICE

16

Quick
+Lib
+Lib
———

17

Lawyer Lawyer
Lawyer Lawyer
Lawyer Lawyer
Lawyer Lawyer
———————
Don't

18

prilifeson
PUNISHMENT

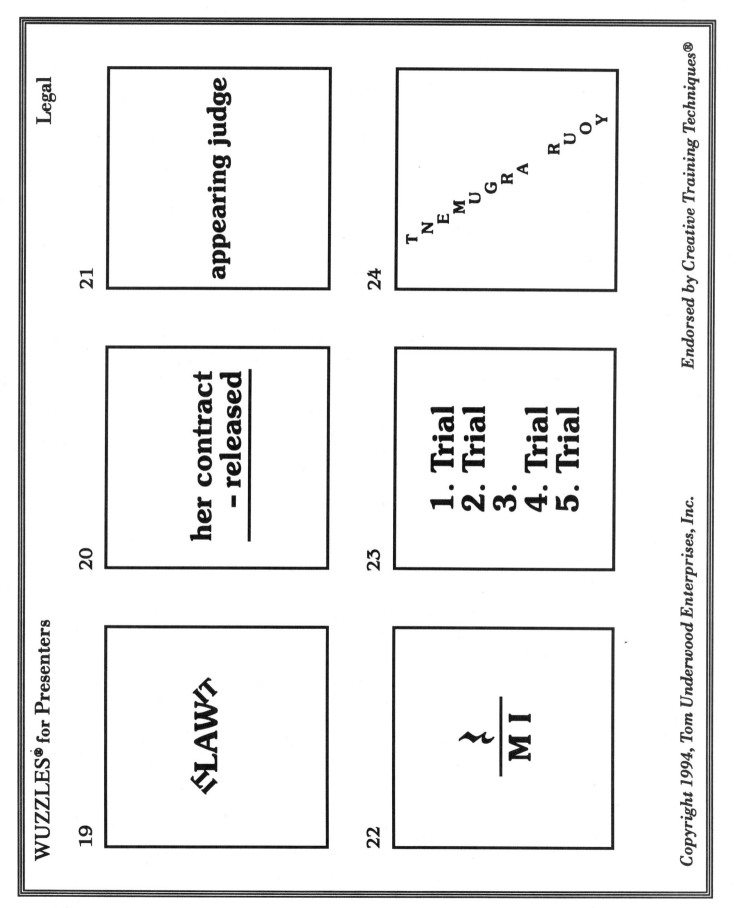

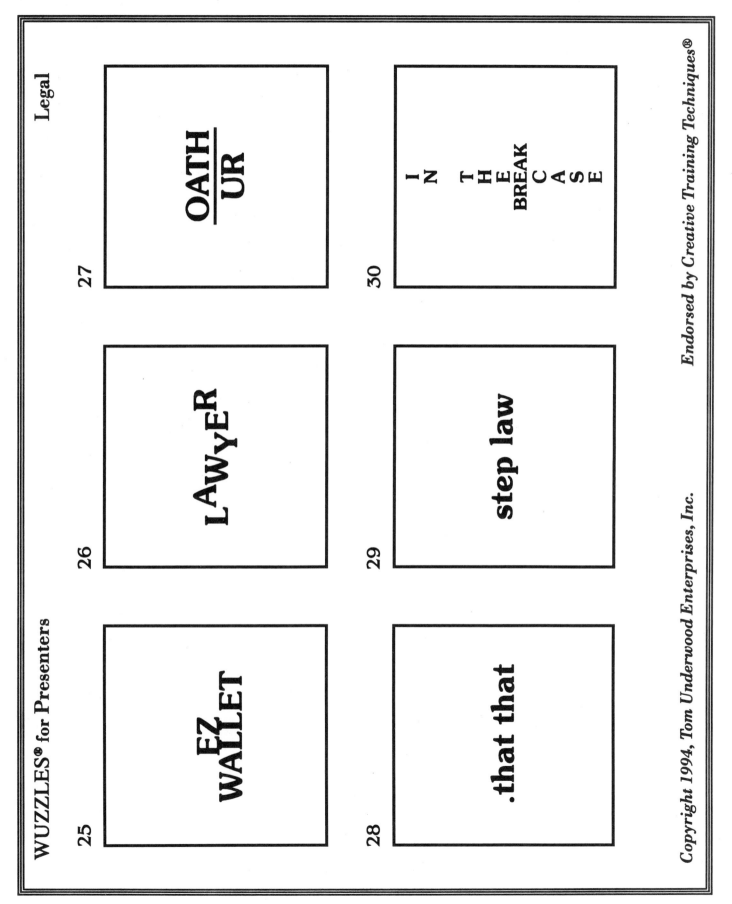

Management

$$\frac{\text{in}}{\text{my head}}$$

Answer: In over my head

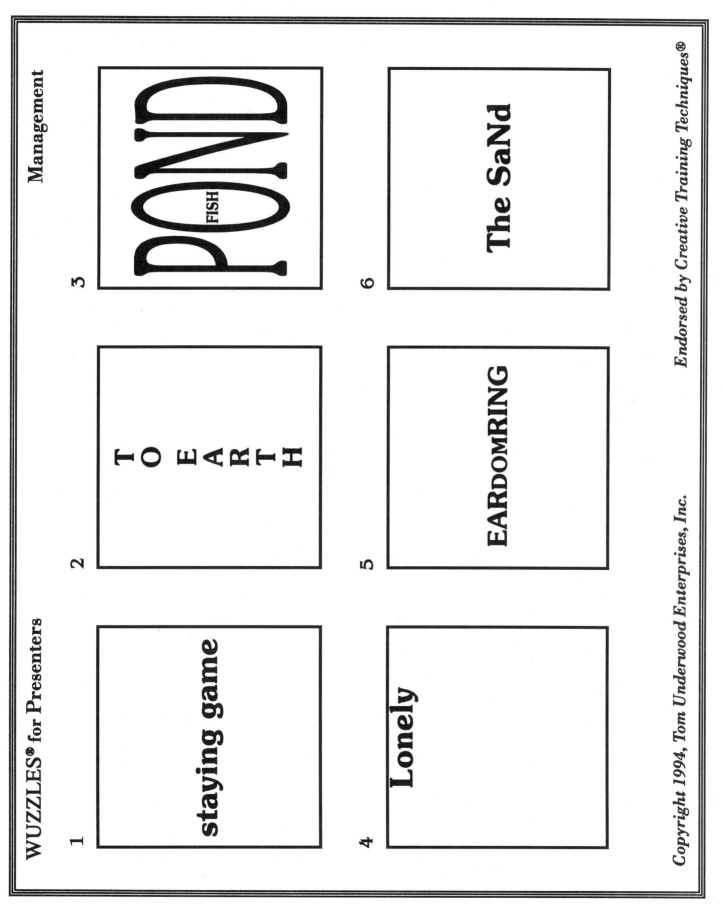

1

staying game

2

T
O
E
A
R
T
H

3

PFISHOND

4

Lonely

5

EAR_{DOM}RING

6

The SaNd

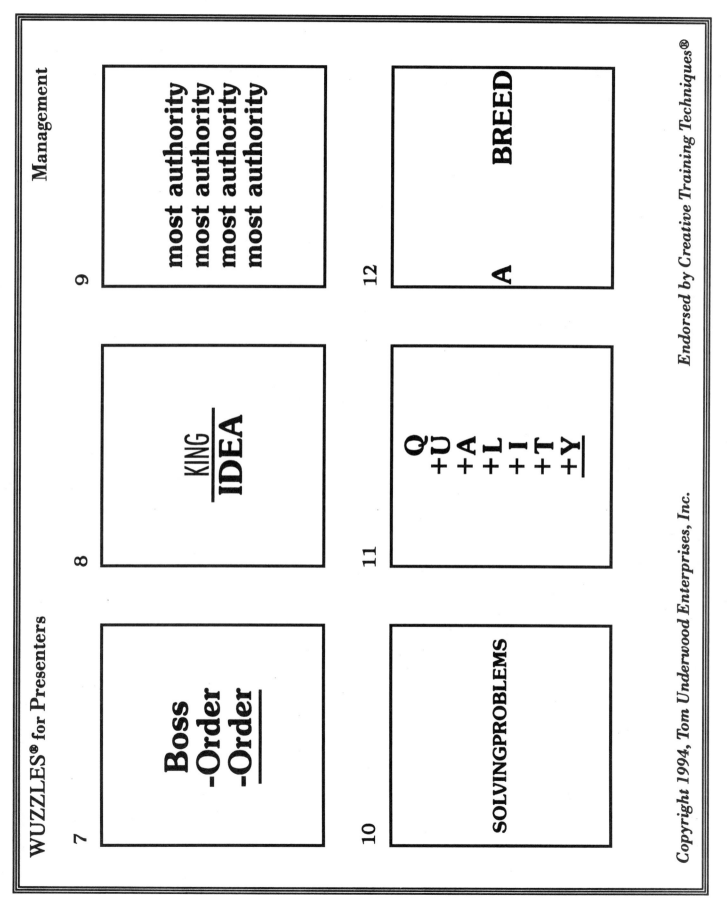

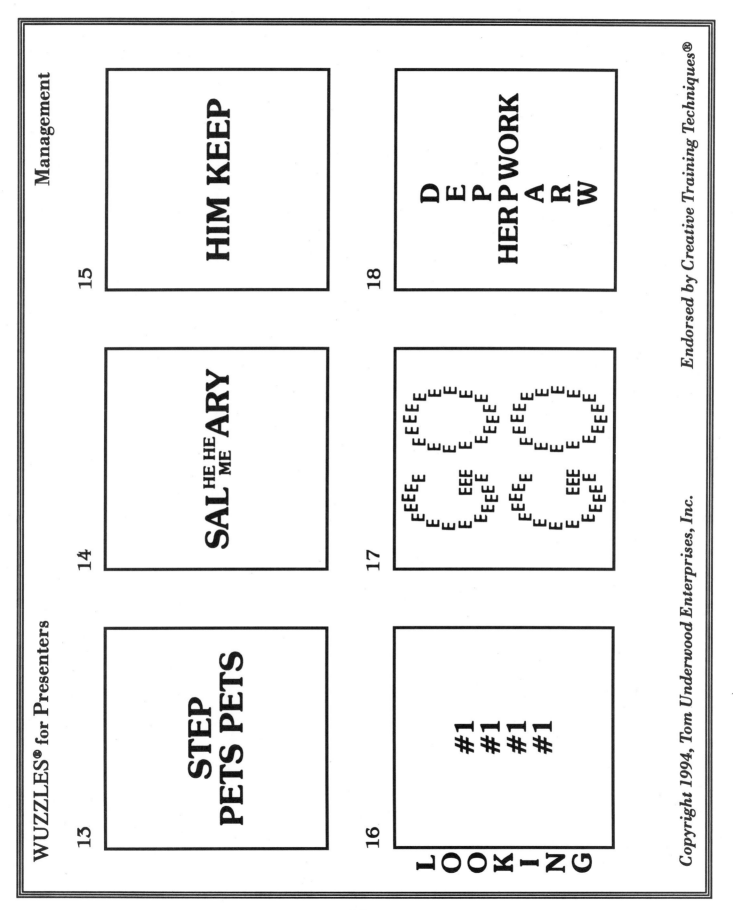

13

STEP
PETS PETS

14

SAL ^{HE HE}_{ME} ARY

15

HIM KEEP

16

#1
#1
#1
#1

L
O
O
K
I
N
G

17

18

D
E
P
HER P WORK
A
R
W

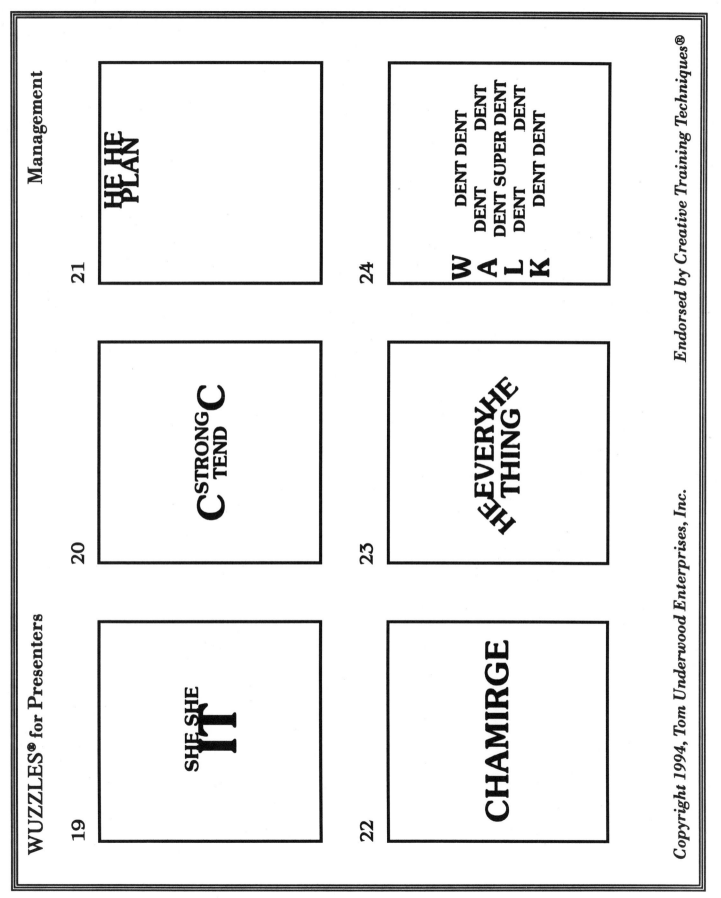

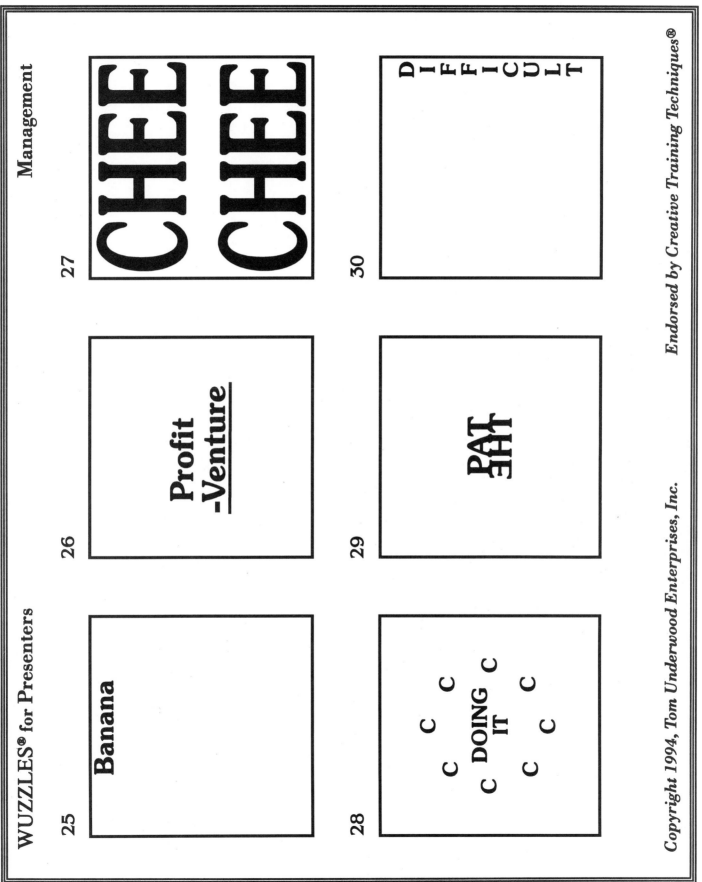

25 Banana

26 Profit
    -Venture

27 CHEE
    CHEE

28 C   C
    C   DOING C
    C   IT
    C   C   C

29 PAT
    THE

30 D
    I
    F
    F
    I
    C
    U
    L
    T

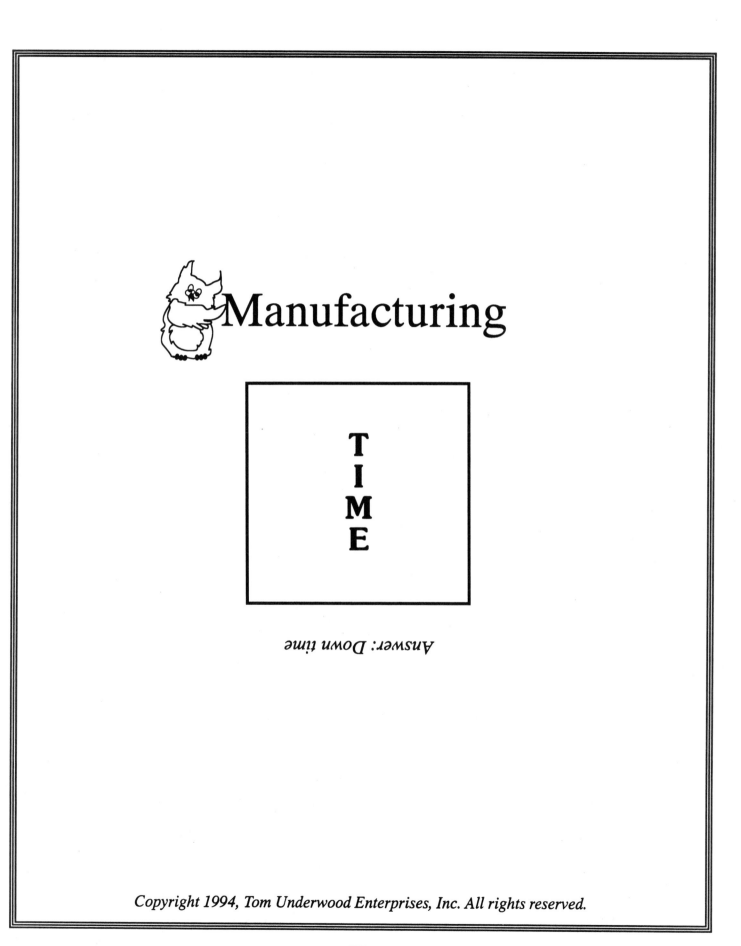

Manufacturing

TIME

Answer: Down time

Manufacturing

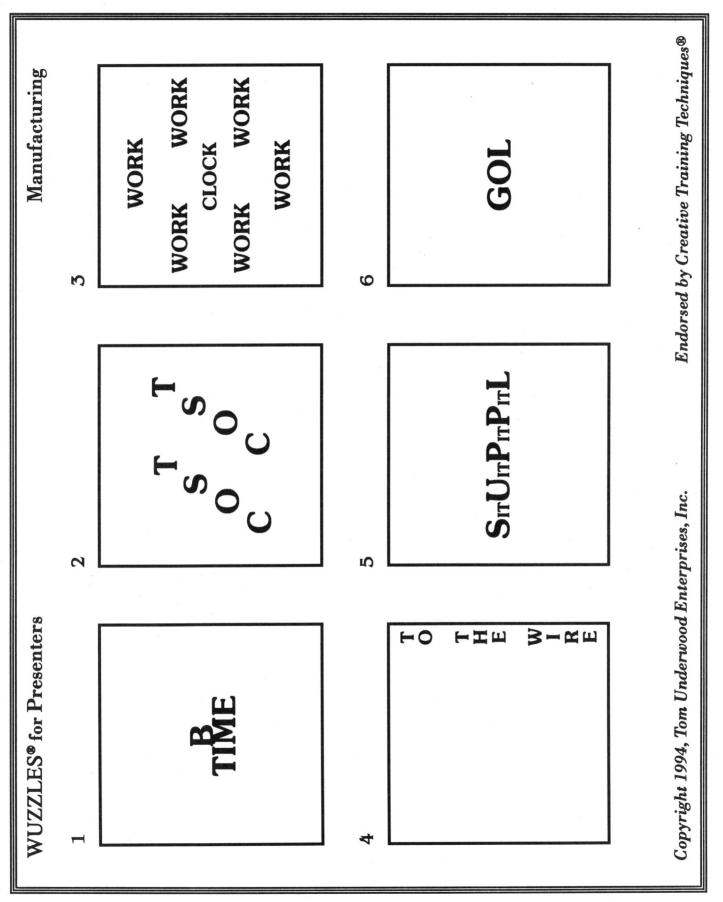

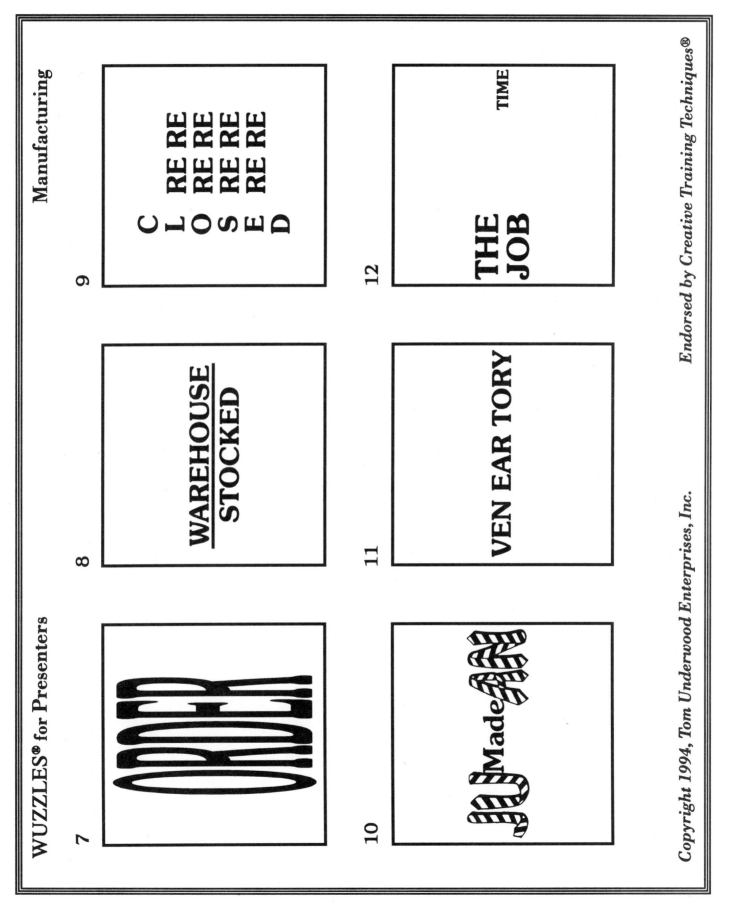

7

8

WAREHOUSE
STOCKED

9

C   RE RE
L   RE RE
O   RE RE
S   RE RE
E   RE RE
D

10

Made

11

VEN EAR TORY

12

THE
JOB

TIME

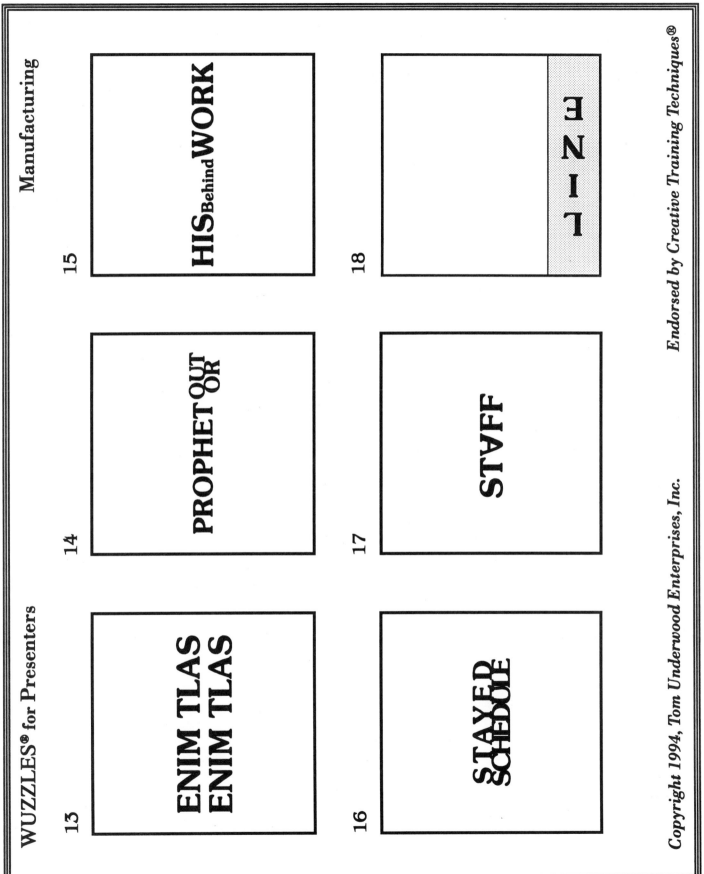

Manufacturing

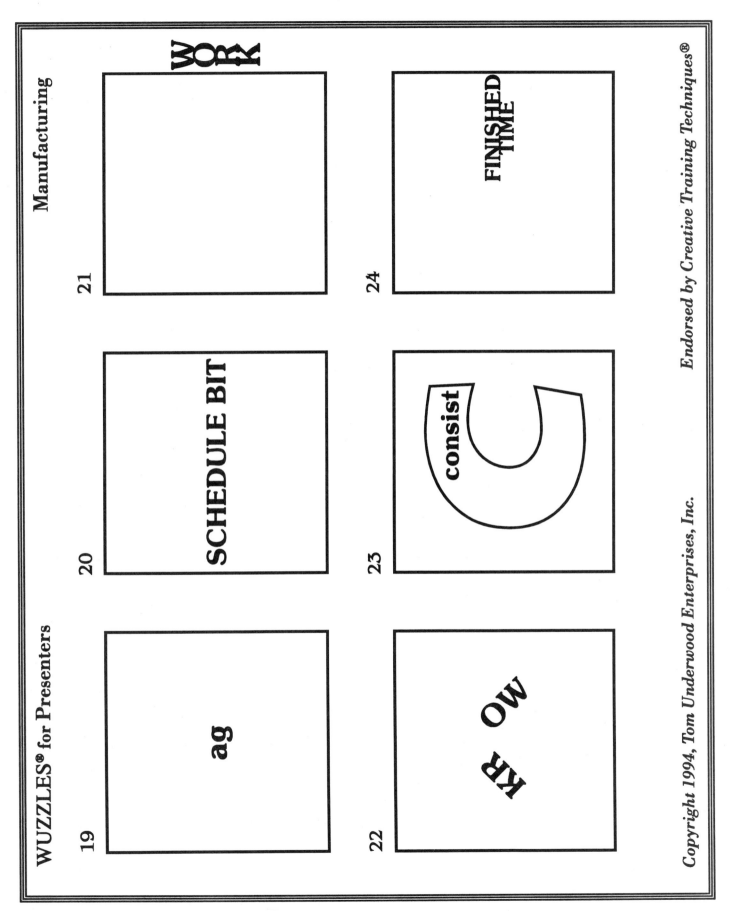

Endorsed by Creative Training Techniques®

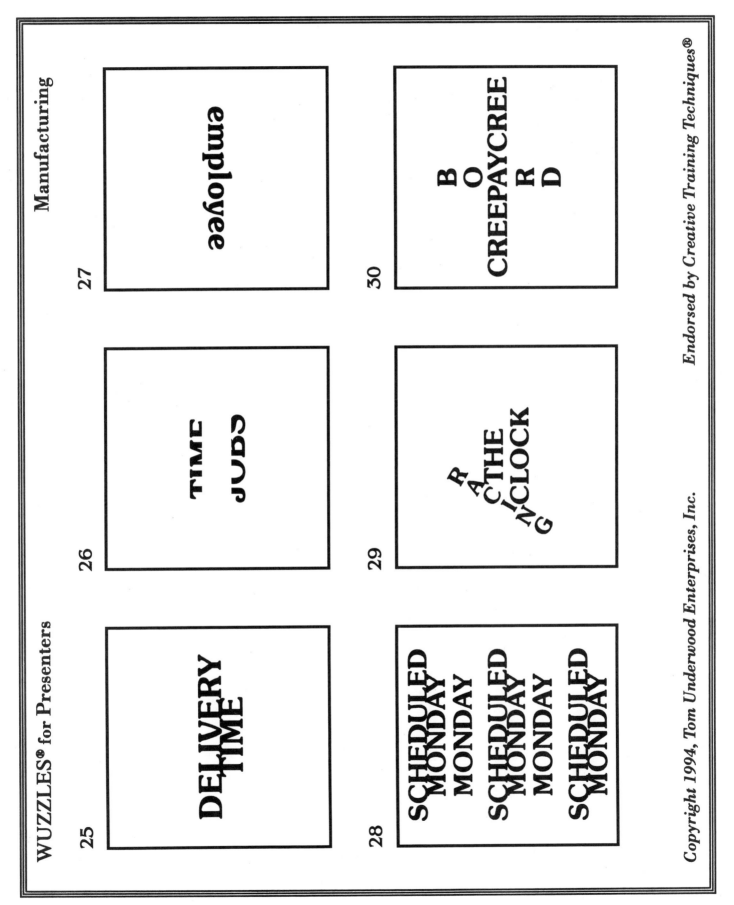

25

DELIVERY
TIME

26

TIME
JOBS

27

employee

28

SCHEDULED
MONDAY
MONDAY
SCHEDULED
MONDAY
MONDAY
SCHEDULED
MONDAY

29

R
A
C THE
N CLOCK
G

30

B
O
CREEPAYCREE
R
D

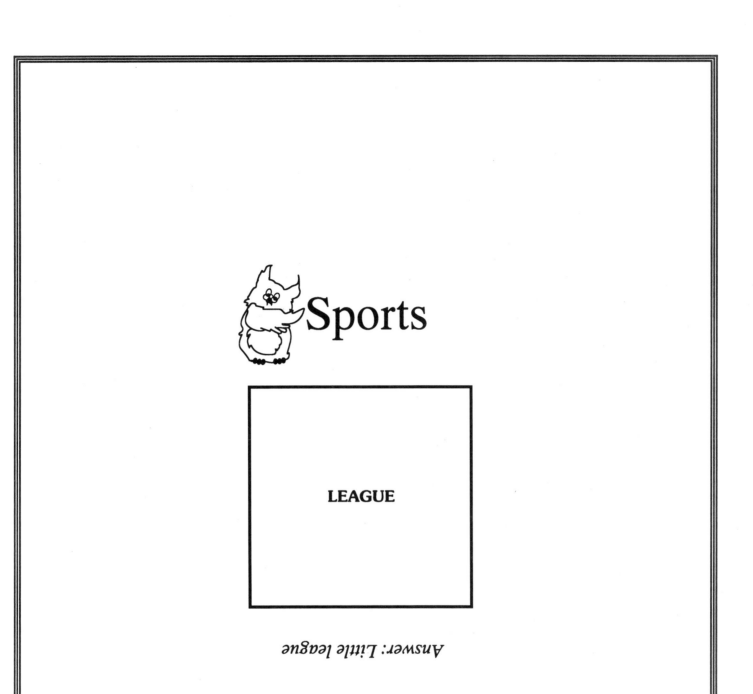

Sports

LEAGUE

Answer: *Little League*

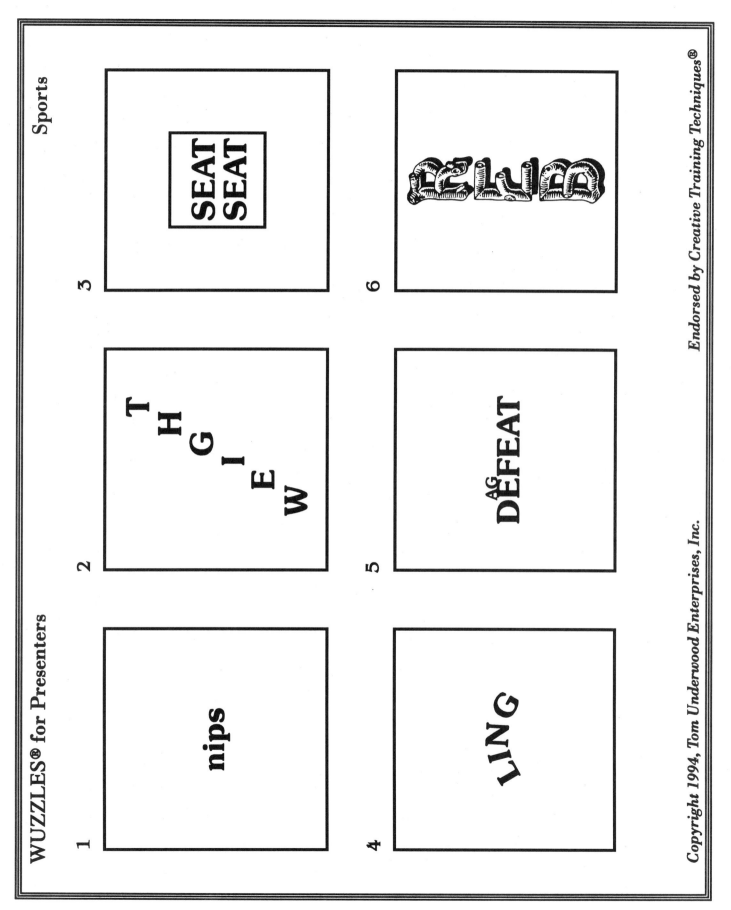

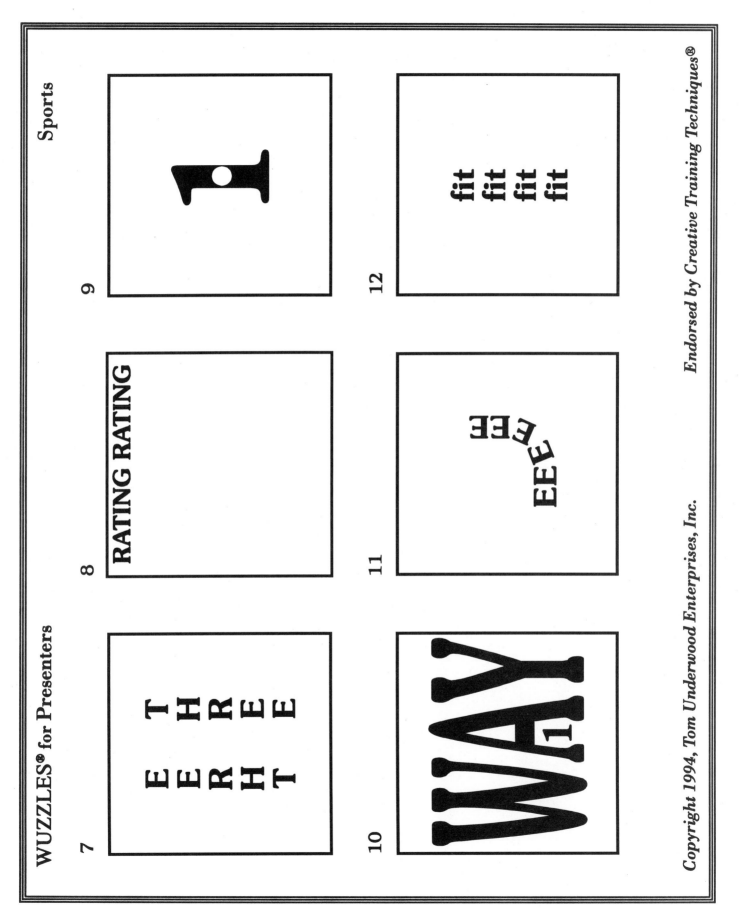

7

E   T
E   H
R   R
H   E
T   E

8

RATING RATING

9

10

WAY₁

11

EE
EEE
EEE

12

fit
fit
fit
fit

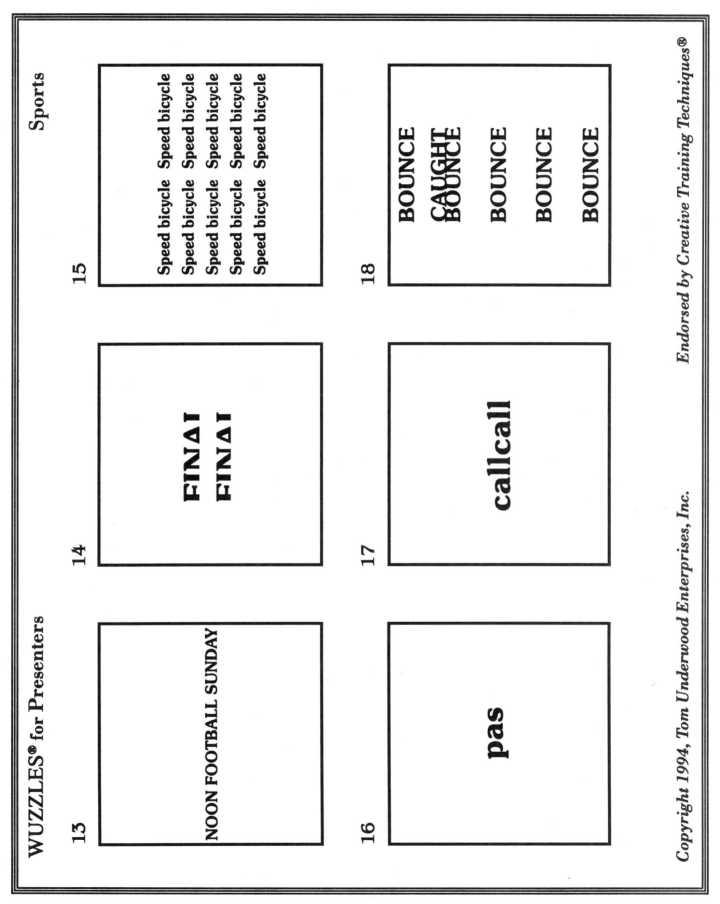

13

NOON FOOTBALL SUNDAY

14

FINAI
FINAI

15

Speed bicycle   Speed bicycle
Speed bicycle   Speed bicycle
Speed bicycle   Speed bicycle
Speed bicycle   Speed bicycle
Speed bicycle   Speed bicycle

16

pas

17

callcall

18

BOUNCE
CAUGHT
BOUNCE
BOUNCE
BOUNCE
BOUNCE

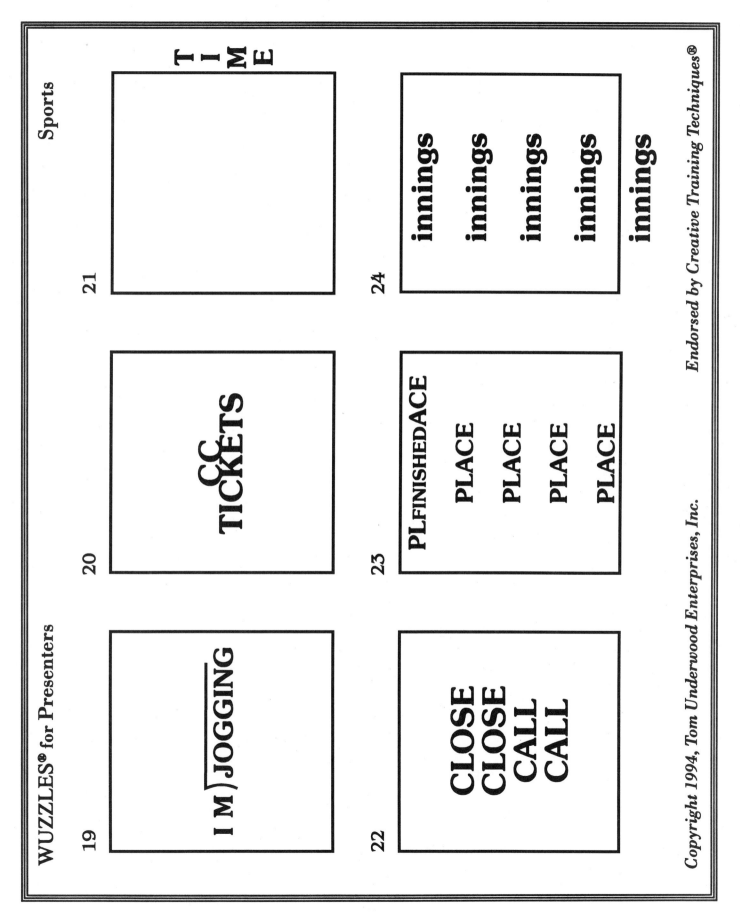

19

I M)JOGGING

20

CC
TICKETS

21

T
I
M
E

22

CLOSE
CLOSE
CALL
CALL

23

PLFINISHEDACE

PLACE

PLACE

PLACE

PLACE

24

innings

innings

innings

innings

innings

Endorsed by Creative Training Techniques®

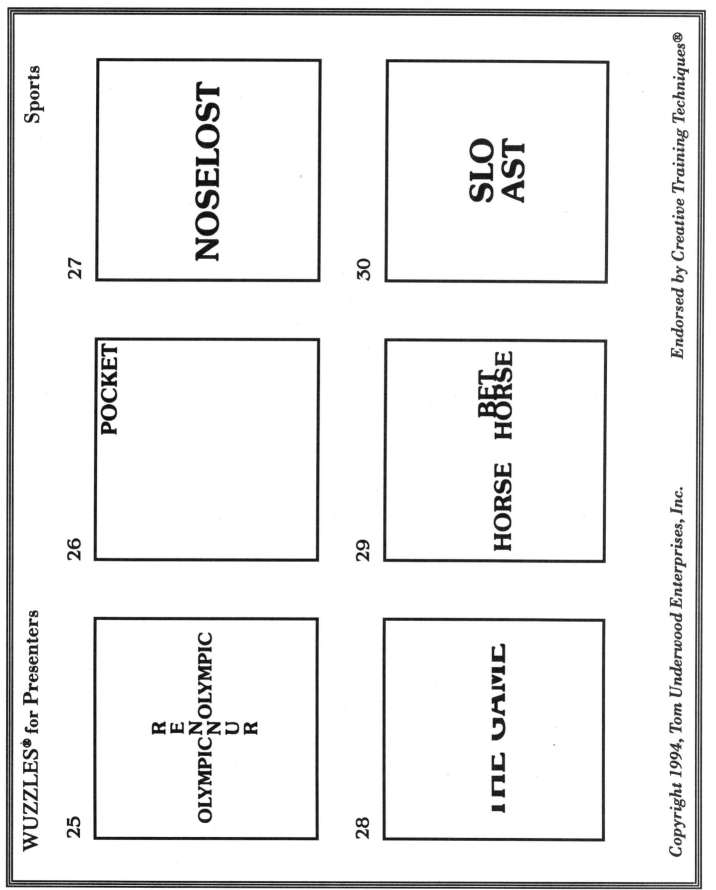

25

R
E
OLYMPIC NOLYMPIC
N U
R

26

POCKET

27

NOSELOST

28

THE GAME

29

HORSE BET HORSE
HORSE

30

SLO
AST

Copyright 1994, Tom Underwood Enterprises, Inc.

Endorsed by Creative Training Techniques®

Technical

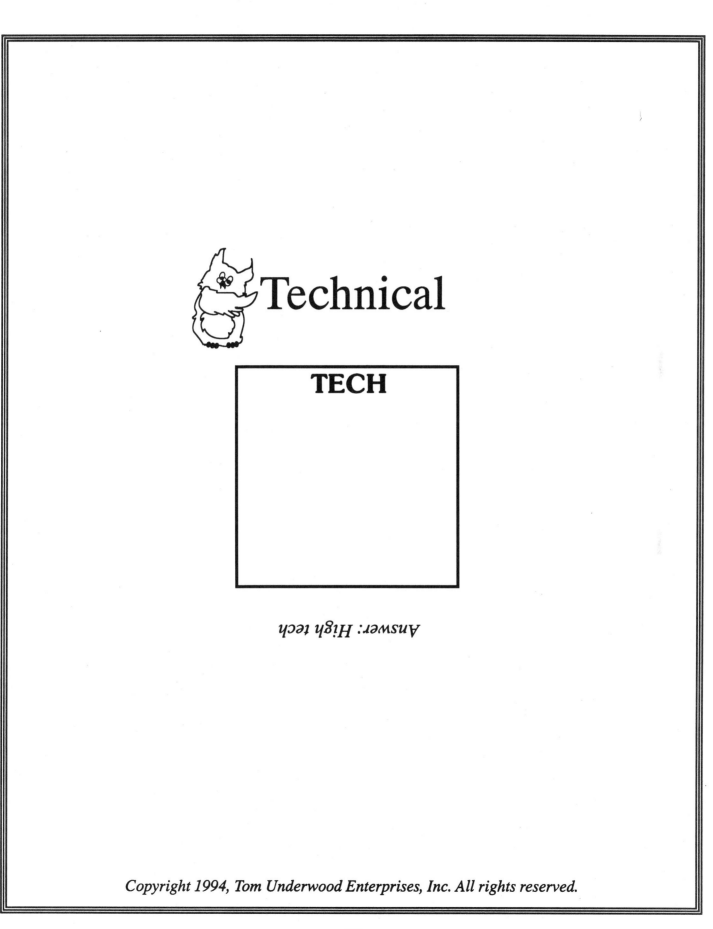

TECH

Answer: High tech

Technical

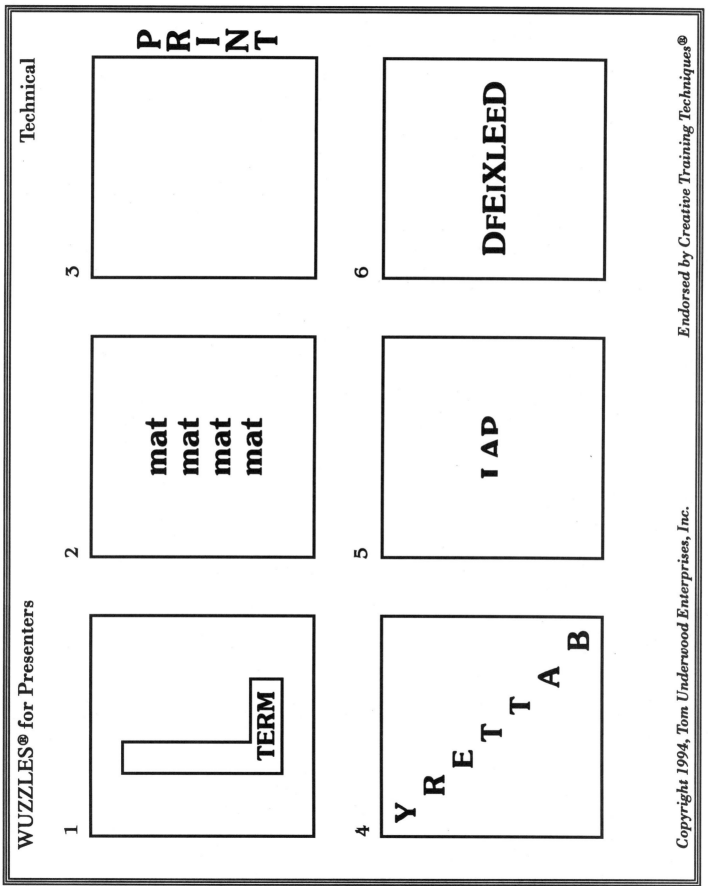

1

2   mat
    mat
    mat
    mat

3   P
    R
    I
    N
    T

4   Y
     R
       E
         T
           T
             A
               B

5   I Λ D

6   DfEiXlEED

Endorsed by Creative Training Techniques®

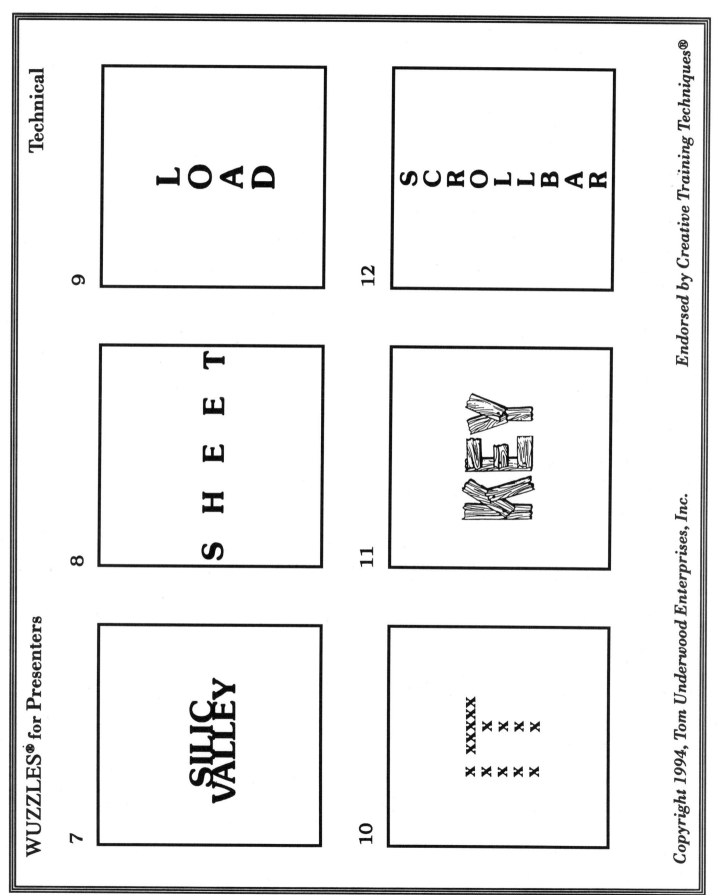

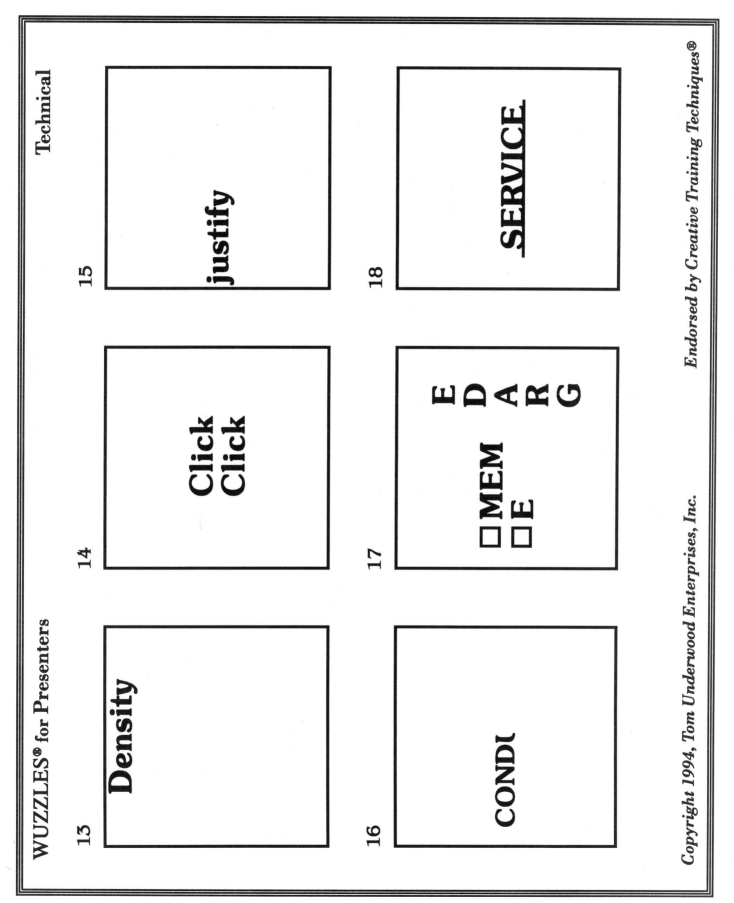

13

Density

14

**Click
Click**

15

justify

16

CONDI

17

□ **MEM** E
□ **E** D
A
R
G

18

SERVICE

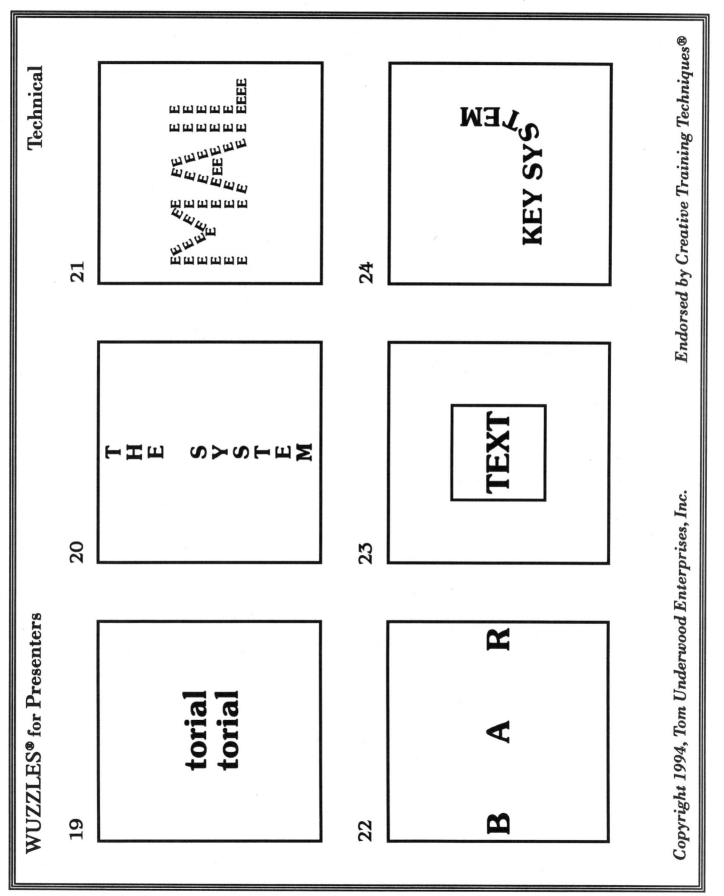

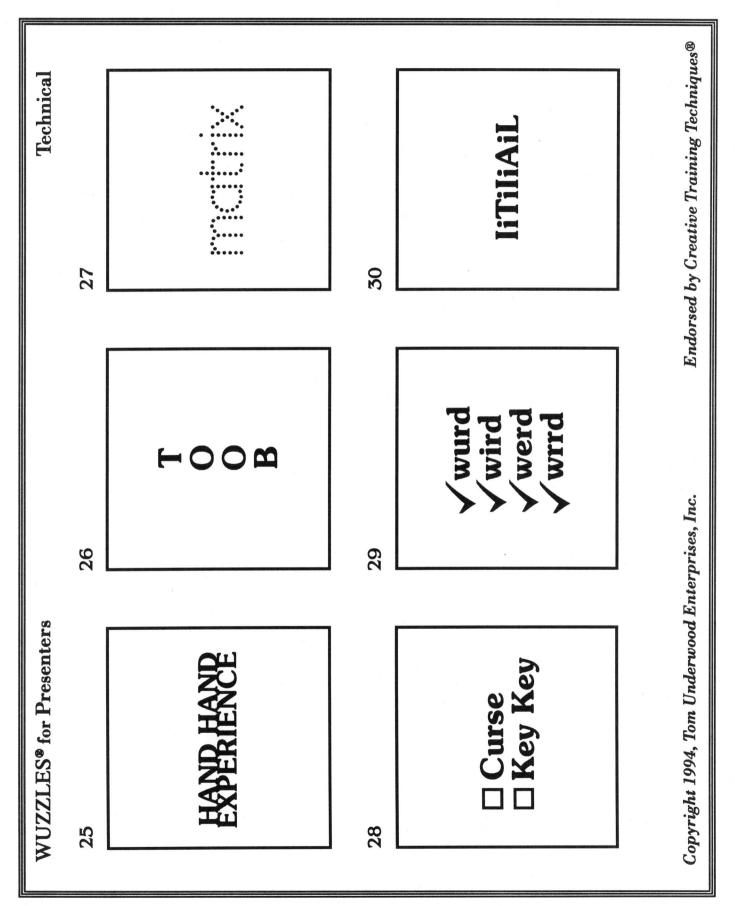

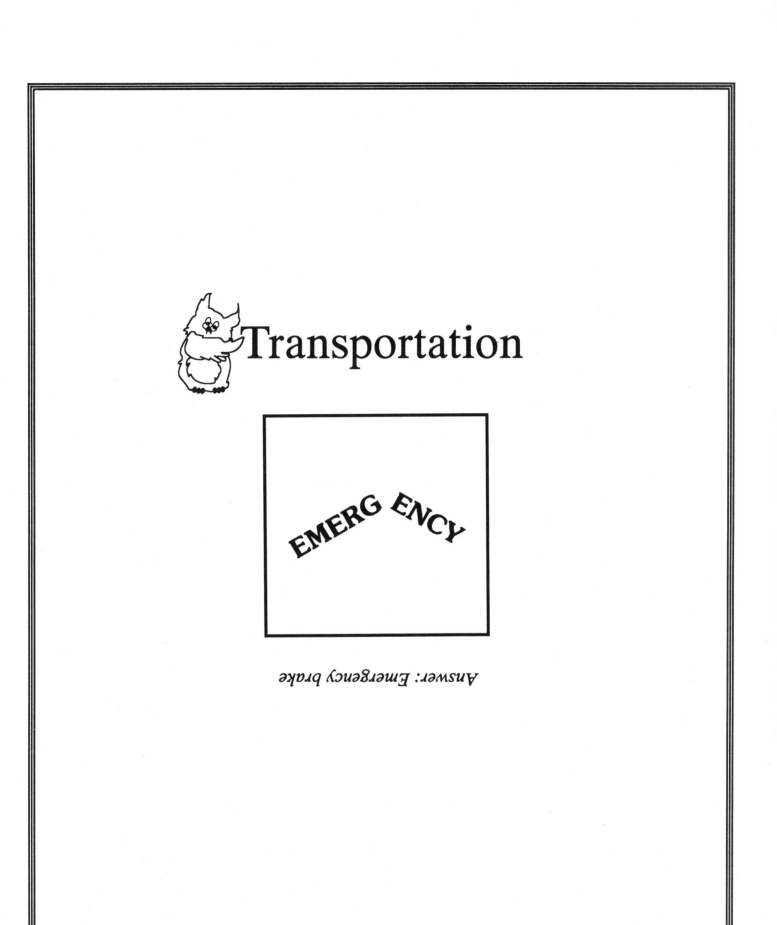

Transportation

EMERG ENCY

Answer: Emergency brake

Transportation

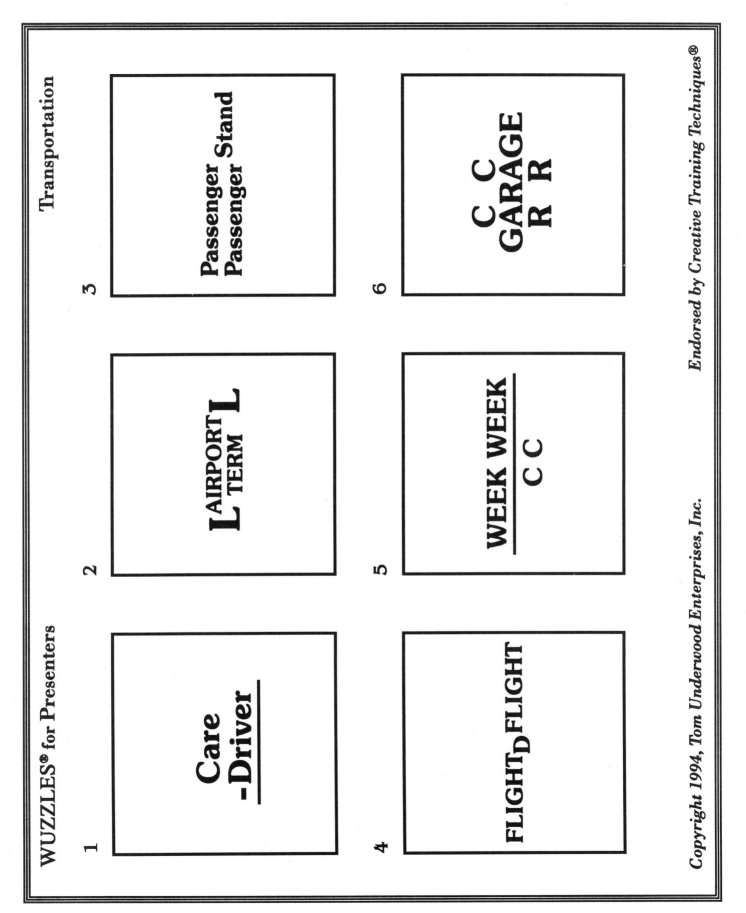

1 Care
-Driver

2 L AIRPORT L
TERM

3 Passenger Stand
Passenger

4 FLIGHT D FLIGHT

5 WEEK WEEK
C C

6 C C
GARAGE
R R

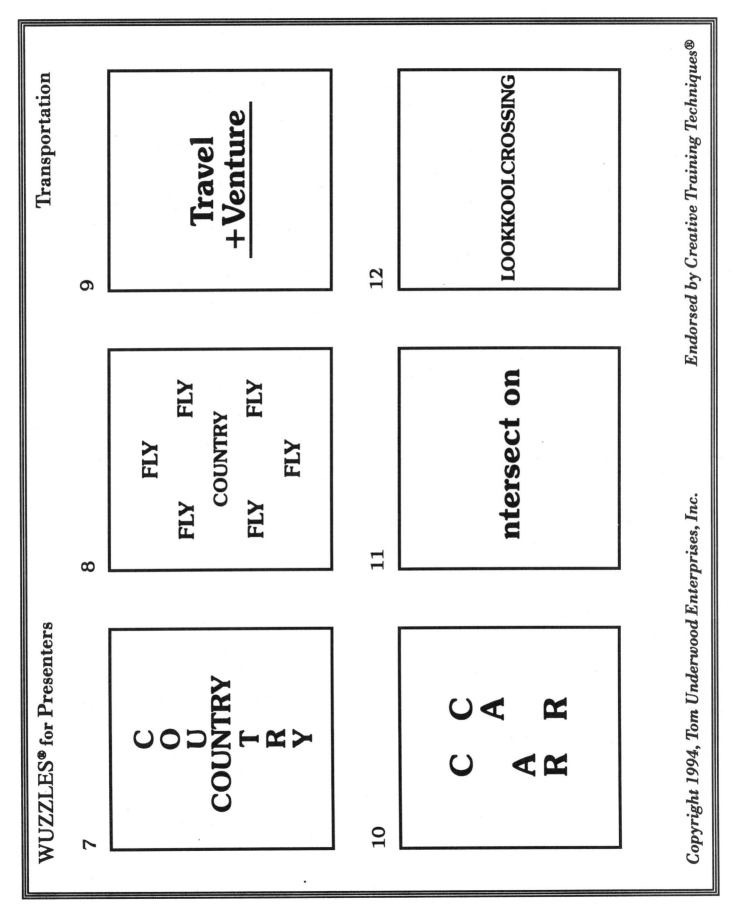

Transportation

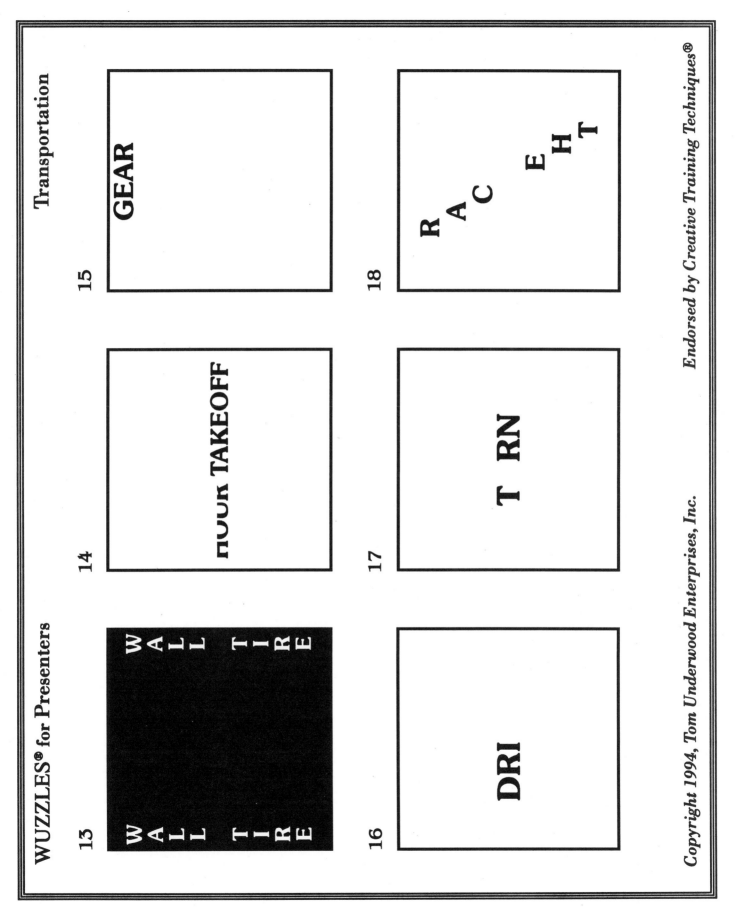

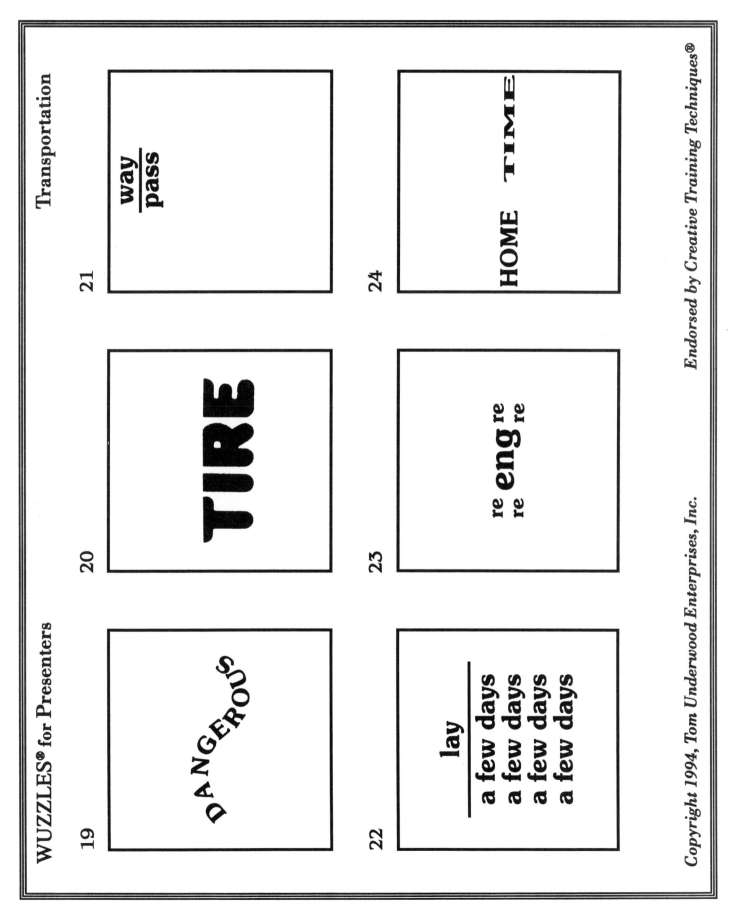

Transportation

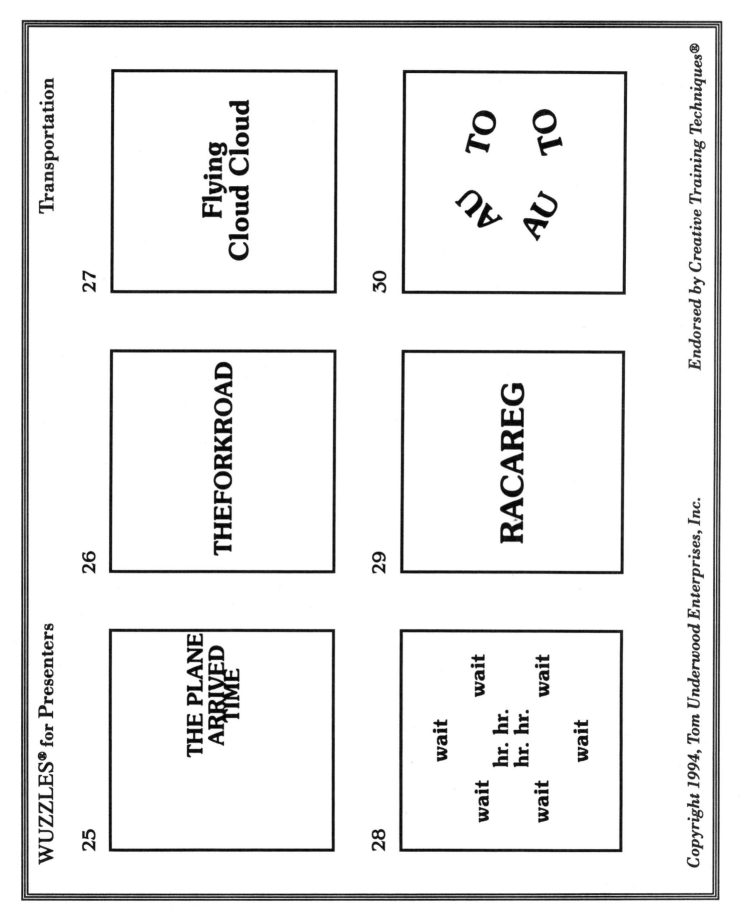

25

26

27 Flying Cloud Cloud

28

29 RACAREG

30

Endorsed by Creative Training Techniques®

Miscellaneous

$$\frac{\textbf{freezing}}{\textbf{just}}$$

Answer: Just below freezing

Miscellaneous

1 world world	2 *RULE RULE*	3 E
4 ravit	5 TALK	6 B E H I N D

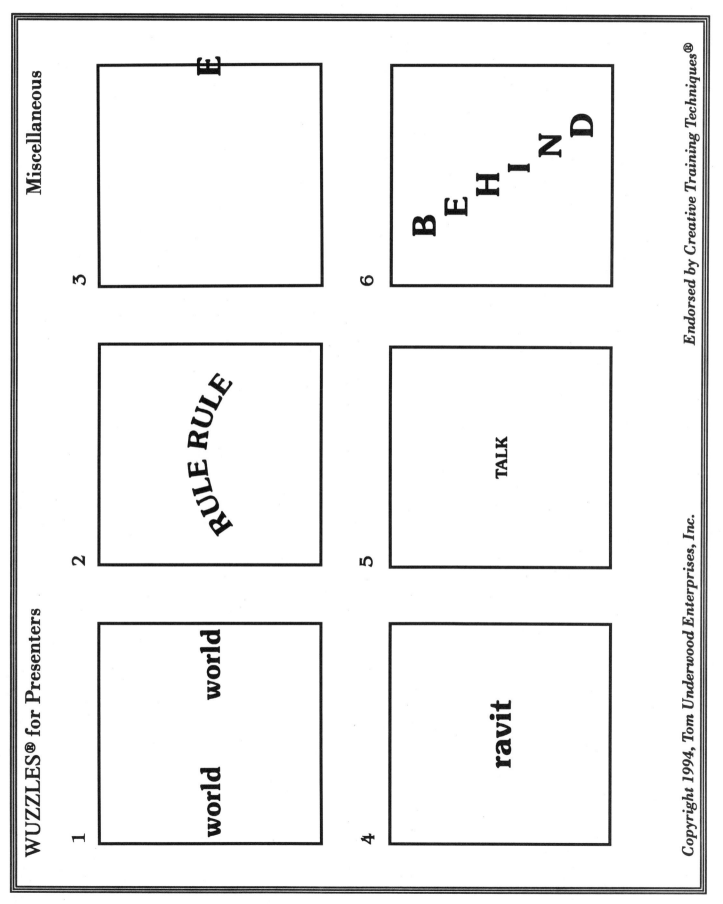

Copyright 1994, Tom Underwood Enterprises, Inc.   *Endorsed by Creative Training Techniques®*

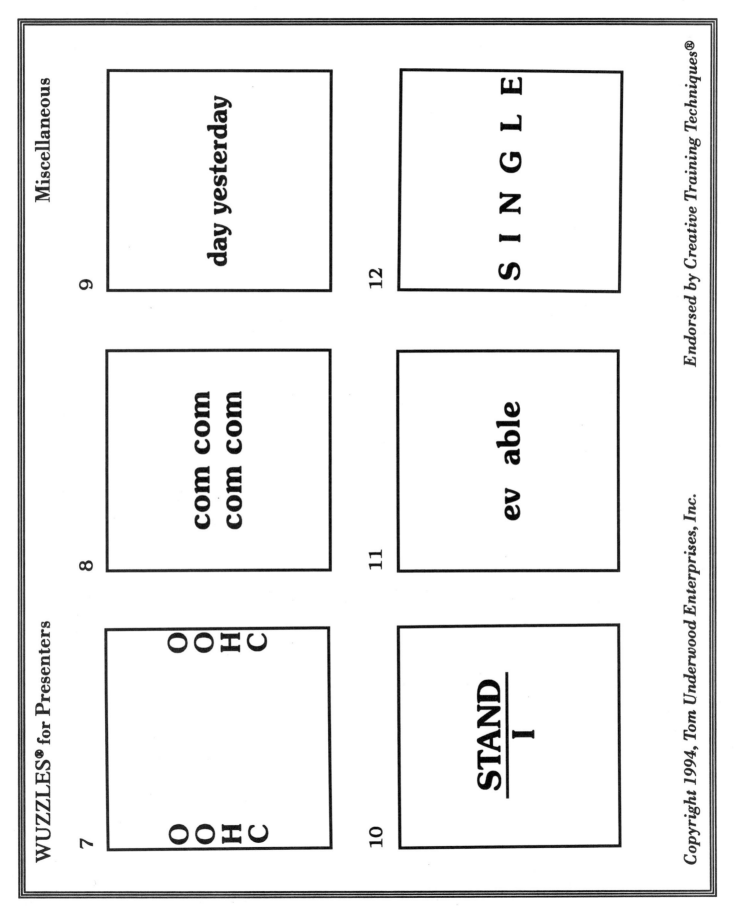

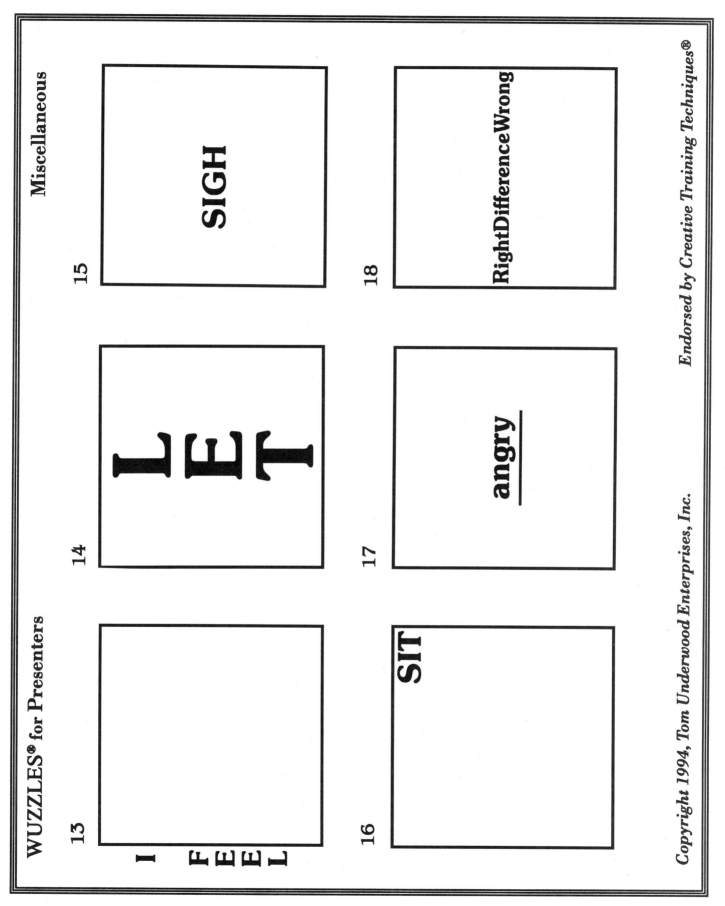

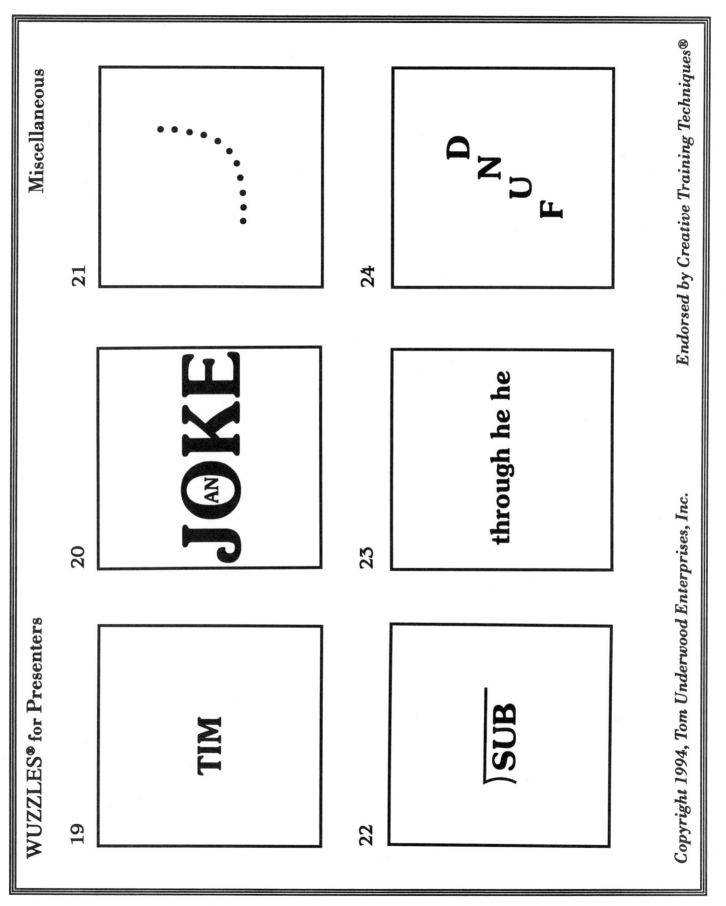

Miscellaneous

19

TIM

20

J〈AN〉KE

21

22

√SUB

23

through he he

24

D
N
U
F

Endorsed by Creative Training Techniques®

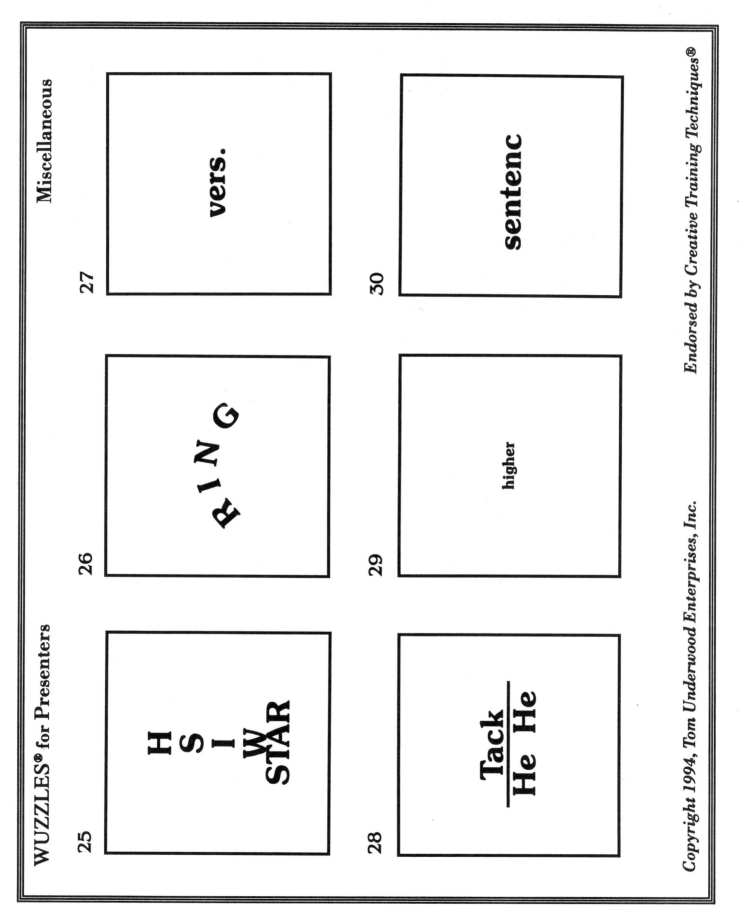

25

H
S
I
W
STAR

26

RING

27

vers.

28

Tack
He He

29

higher

30

sentenc

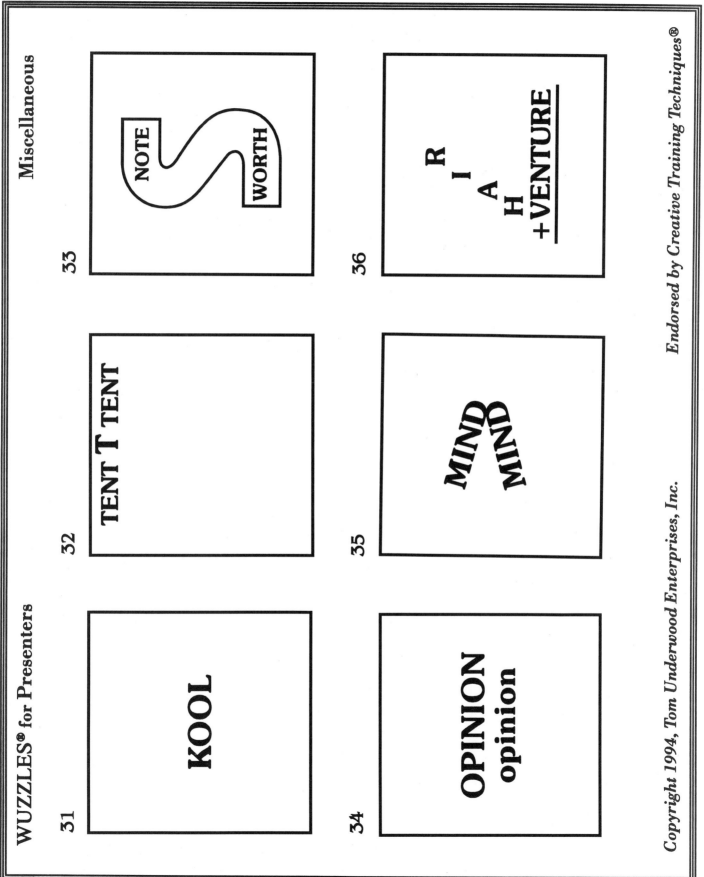

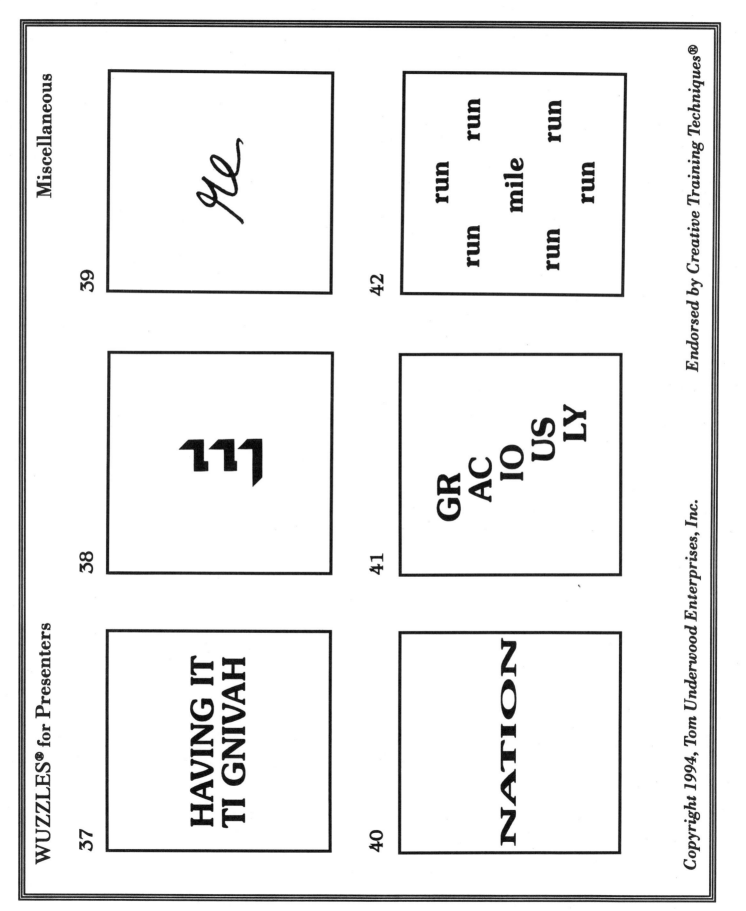

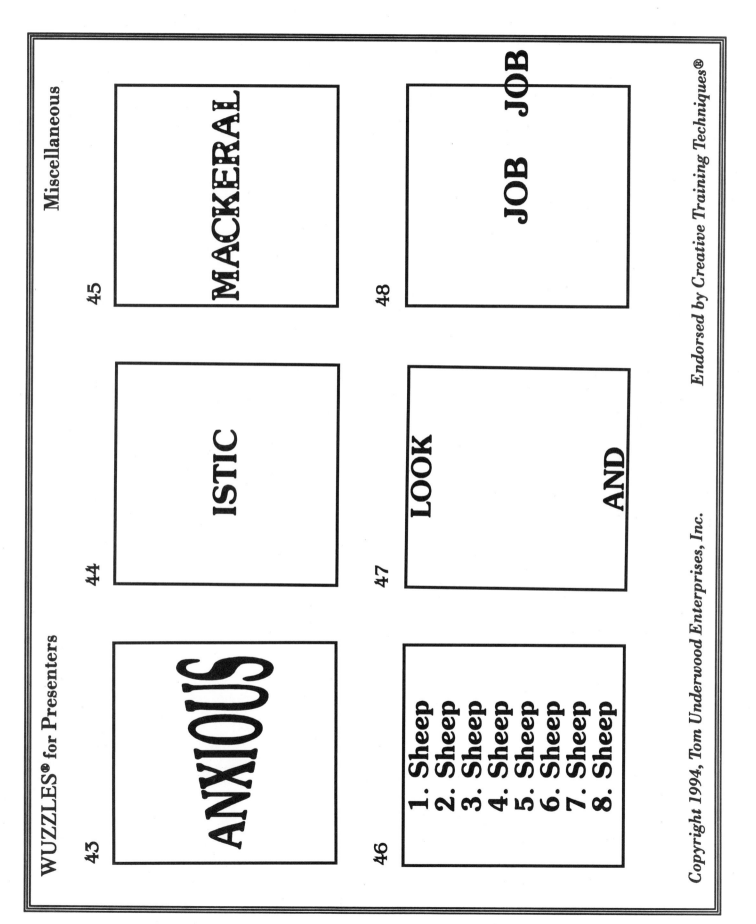

43

ANXIOUS

44

ISTIC

45

MACKERAL

46

1. Sheep
2. Sheep
3. Sheep
4. Sheep
5. Sheep
6. Sheep
7. Sheep
8. Sheep

47

LOOK

AND

48

JOB   JOB

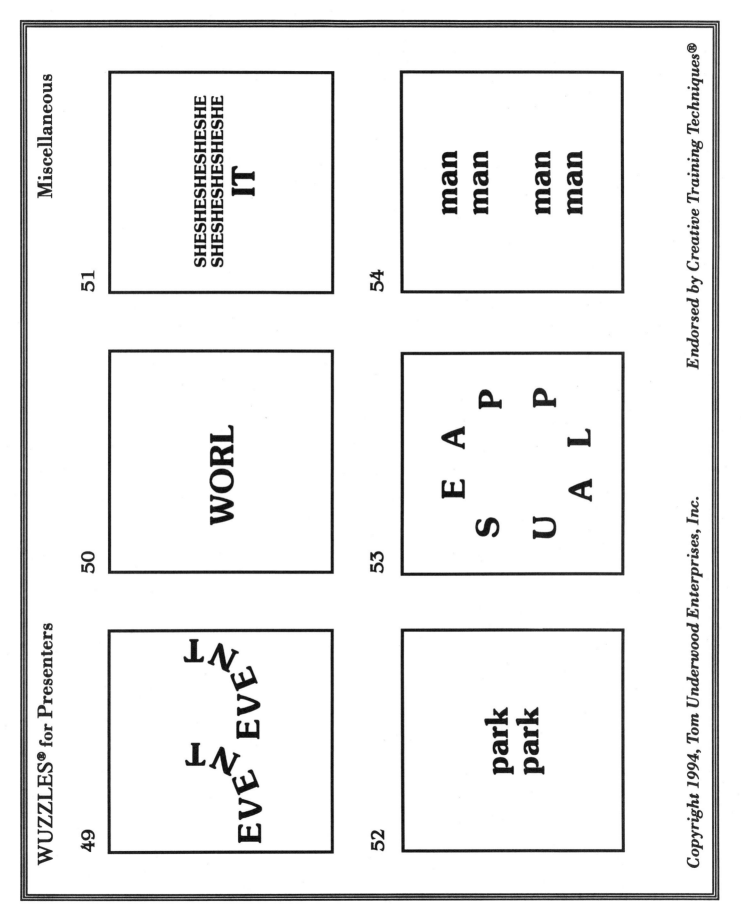

Miscellanous

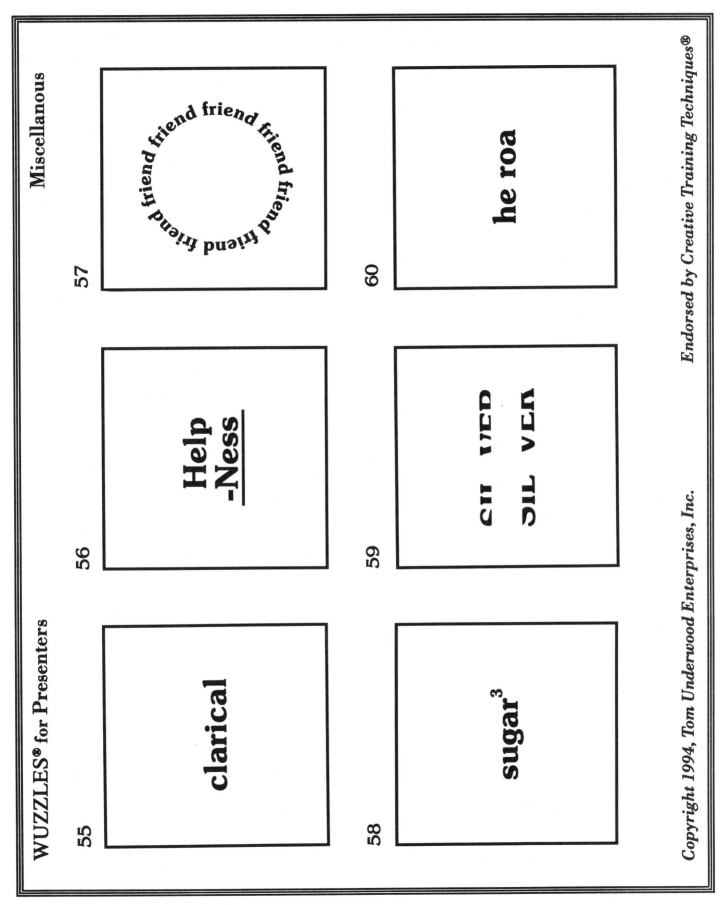

55 clarical

56 Help
    -Ness

57 friend friend friend friend friend friend friend friend friend friend friend friend friend friend

58 sugar³

59 CIT VED
    SIL VER

60 he roa

Endorsed by Creative Training Techniques®

89

Biography of the Author

TOM UNDERWOOD

It can be said that Tom Underwood is a very puzzling person. During the past 30 years, he has created 13 different forms of puzzles that have appeared in newspapers and magazines throughout the United States and in several foreign countries.

Tom's most successful puzzle creation is Wuzzles®, a newspaper feature which is distributed throughout the world by King Features Syndicate. Because of syndication, Wuzzles® are now seen by 6 ½ million people every day.

Wuzzles® began as a party game in 1971 (with only 200 Wuzzles® in the collection), became a local newspaper feature in 1982, and went into syndication in 1985. There are more than 10,000 Wuzzles® in the Underwood computer files.

Tom was a teacher, coach, and school administrator before retiring from education in 1994. He now spends most of his time doing things that will puzzle many of us.

ROBERT W. PIKE, CSP

Robert has developed and implemented training programs for business, industry, government and the professions since 1969. As president of Resources for Organizations, Inc., Creative Training Techniques International, Inc., and The Resources Group, Inc., Bob leads sessions over 150 days per year covering topics of leadership, attitudes, motivation, communication, decision-making, problem-solving, personal and organizational effectiveness, conflict management, team building and managerial productivity. More than 50,000 trainers have attended the Creative Training Techniques® workshop. As a consultant, Bob has worked with such organizations as Pfizer, UpJohn, Caesar Boardwalk Regency, Exhibitor Magazine, Hallmark Cards, Inc. and IBM.

Over the years Bob has contributed to magazines like "Training," "The Personal Administrator" and "The Self-Development Journal." He is editor of the "Creative Training Techniques Newsletter" and is author of "The Creative Training Techniques Handbook," "Developing, Marketing and Promoting Successful Seminars and Workshops" and "Improving Managerial Productivity."

WIN *Rave Reviews*
on your next **Presentation**

"I have never felt so enthusiastic about a program! This workshop is a MUST for any trainer, regardless of level of experience."

Susan Russell, Bank One

Do you talk so people really listen?

Bob Pike's Creative Training Techniques™ Seminar

Find out why over 65,000 trainers love Creative Training Techniques. What makes this seminar so different? You'll learn how to get your participants enthusiastically involved in the training. By creating an interactive learning environment, you'll watch the attendees excitement go up and up and up. The result? Your group will easily learn twice as much. When they apply their new skills on the job, you'll see dramatic results.

Learn a revolutionary training approach—Participant-Centered Training. This teaching style is far more effective than traditional lecture-based training. Over 65,000 trainers world-wide have attended this seminar and applied these participant-centered training techniques to their work environments. More effective training means a more valuable and effective work force. Register today so you can get rave reviews on your next presentation. Over 140 public seminars are scheduled in 40 different cities each year.

In-house Training Seminars

Customized programs for trainers, sales staff, and technical presenters developed for 100s of organizations. Give us a call so we can discuss how to help your company increase work force performance by maximizing the impact of your training. Just a few of our clients who have brought Creative Training Techniques programs in-house:

American Express • AT&T • GE Plastics • State Farm Insurance • 3M • Tonka Corporation

Creative Solutions Catalog
Insider's Tips to Double the Impact of Your Presentation

Filled with fun, stimulating, creative resources including games, magic, music, wuzzles, books, tapes, videos, software, presentation graphics—everything you need to make your presentation an absolute winner.

1-800-383-9210
www.cttbobpike.com

Creative Training Techniques International, Inc. • 7620 W. 78th Street, Mpls. MN 55439 • (612) 829-1954 • Fax (612) 829-0260

Bob Pike's

Creative Training Techniques™
Train-the-Trainer Conference

*The only conference dedicated exclusively
to the participant-centered approach to training*

- Learn about the revolutionary, participant-centered training approach—the breakthrough alternative to lecture-based training
- See the nation's leading training consultants model their very best participant-centered activities
- Experience the power of participant-centered techniques to dramatically increase retention
- Learn about innovative training transfer techniques adopted by leading Fortune 500 companies
- Discover powerful management strategies that clearly demonstrate the business results for your training programs

Just a few of the companies who have sent groups (not just individuals) to the Conference

American Express • AT&T • Caterpillar • First Bank
Southern Nuclear Operating Company • State Farm • United HealthCare • US West

Rave Reviews!

"I refer to my conference workbook all the time. I've shared the techniques with my trainers, and my own evaluations have improved. Our needs analysis now produces actionable input. My comfort level with our line managers has increased—at my first meeting with them where I used what I learned at the conference, they applauded. Now that's positive feedback!"
Gretchen Gospodarek, Training Manager, **TCF Bank Wisconsin**

"For any trainer who wants to move beyond lecture-based training, I recommend Bob Pike's participant-centered seminars and in-house consultants."
Ken Blanchard, Co-Author of *The One-Minute Manager*

"Bob Pike is creating a new standard in the industry by which all other programs will soon be measured."

Elliott Masie, President, **The MASIE Center**

Visit our Web site: www.cttbobpike.com to learn more about the Conference,
Creative Training Techniques International, Inc. or the Participant-Centered Training approach.

[CTT logo]

1–800–383–9210
www.cttbobpike.com

Creative Training Techniques International, Inc. • 7620 W. 78th St., Mpls., MN 55439 • 612-829-1954 • Fax 612-829-0260

13 Questions to Ask *Before* You Bring Anyone In-House

An in-house program is an investment. You want to ensure high return. Here are 13 questions to ask before you ask anyone to train your trainers (or train anyone else!).

1. What kind of measurable results have other clients had from your training?
2. How much experience does this company have in training trainers?
3. Is this 100 percent of what the company does or just part of what it does?
4. How experienced are the trainers who will work with our people?
5. How experienced are your trainers in maximizing training transfer to the job?
6. Is the program tailored to my needs, or is it the same content as the public program?
7. Why is an in-house program to our advantage?
8. Is team-building a by-product of the seminar?
9. Is there immediate application of new skills during the training session?
10. What kinds of resource and reference materials do we get?
11. What type of pre-course preparation or post-course follow-up do you do?
12. How are our participants recognized for their achievements?
13. Will you teach my trainers how to get participant buy-in, even from the difficult participant?

Advantages of a Customized, In-House Program with Creative Training Techniques™ International, Inc.

Customized in-house programs provide your organization with training tailored to your specific needs. Our unique participant-centered teaching style is a revolutionary new training approach that is far more effective than traditional lecture-based training. This training approach has been adapted by a wide range of industries including healthcare, finance, communications, government, and non-profit agencies. Our clients include American Express, AT&T, Hewlett-Packard, 3M, U.S. Healthcare, and Tonka Corporation. We are eager to learn about your training needs and discuss how we can provide solutions. Please give us a call so we can help your company create a more vital and effective workforce.

[CTT logo]

1–800–383–9210
www.cttbobpike.com

Creative Training Techniques International, Inc. • 7620 W. 78th St., Mpls., MN 55439 • 612-829-1954 • Fax 612-829-0260

Answers to WUZZLES®

Business/Sales pgs. 2-6

1. It's down in price
2. Cheaper by the dozen
3. Back orders
4. A part-time job or
   Time away from the job
5. Pays through the nose
6. Getting down to business
7. Closed on holidays
8. Corner the market
9. A little improvement over last year
10. Incorporate
11. The inside track
12. Wholesale
13. Sold it with ease
14. Needless expense
15. Archrivals
16. Business ties
17. Working after hours
18. Semiannual report
19. Vicious circle
20. Fringe benefits
21. Net income
22. A little bit overextended
23. Price list
24. Looking around for bargains
25. The check's in the mail
26. Think big
27. Bare bones
28. Added pressures
29. High turnover
30. He's back in business

Communications pgs. 8-12

1. Speak up
2. Kicks around the idea
3. Feedback
4. High point of the session
5. Extrovert
6. Broken English
7. Bulletin boards
8. Begin on cue
9. Rough draft
10. Keep it between you two
11. Back after a short message
12. Handwritten
13. Shoot from the hip
14. Written up in the newspaper
15. After-dinner speech or A
   speech after dinner
16. The middle of a conversation
17. Mixed messages
18. Speaks with an accent
19. Fill in the blanks
20. Information gap
21. Two-way conversation
22. Spread the word
23. Think twice before speaking
24. A part of speech
25. A bigmouth
26. Turn up the radio
27. Backtalk
28. Written down on paper
29. Asinine questions
30. Endless chatter

Customer Service pgs. 14-18

1. Going above and beyond
2. Marked down
3. Common courtesy
4. Bending over backwards to please
5. Top-level service
6. Don't buy it
7. A little misunderstanding
8. Pretty please, with sugar on it
9. No surprises
10. Invest in doing it right
11. There is no second chance
12. Meeting deadlines
13. Growing awareness
14. Return customers
15. Warranty
16. The customer needs you
17. Comparison shopping
18. Customers are always right
19. Service after the sale
20. Get your act together
21. High expectations
22. Good intentions
23. Always listen
24. Lowering prices or Falling prices
25. Caring about customers
26. Broken contract
27. Comes across well
28. Rub the wrong way
29. Condescending
30. Please step up to the counter

Education pgs. 20-24

1. English lessons
2. Learn-by-doing
3. School boards
4. Eight periods in the school day
5. I before E, except after C
6. A report card without an A
7. Stays after school
8. Learning curve
9. Pen in hand
10. Far above average intelligence
11. Back to basics
12. High grades in school
13. History prof
14. Hangs around school
15. Guesses right
16. Continuing education
17. A list of courses
18. Cutting classes
19. High school ring
20. Cross references
21. School's out
22. Transcript
23. Foreign language
24. Circle the correct answer
25. Stay in school
26. Knowledge gap
27. Seminar
28. Decreasing attendance
29. He has it in for teachers
30. Extracurricular

Finance/Banking pgs 26-30

1. Salary after taxes
2. Flat broke
3. Foreign currency
4. Double-digit inflation
5. Bank liens
6. A check at the end of the month
7. A little extra income
8. Inflationary spiral
9. Break even
10. He's down to the last dollar
11. Branch bank
12. Extra money on the side
13. A little overdrawn
14. Pennies from heaven
15. A balanced checkbook
16. Write checks
17. Capital gains
18. Nothing in the bank
19. A long-term mortgage
20. Time-and-a-half
21. Live high on the hog
22. Desperately low on funds
23. Forgeries
24. A blank check
25. Shrinking savings
26. Due on the first of the month
27. A big spender
28. Overdue bills or Bills overdue
29. Foreign exchange
30. Low downpayment

Government pgs. 32-36

1. Takes over the job
2. Raising salaries
3. Crooked politicians
4. United we stand, divided we fall
5. Archives
6. Absentee ballot
7. Let freedom ring
8. Write-in candidates
9. Long-winded
10. Attorney General
11. Separation of powers
12. Tomorrow's elections
13. Stand up for your rights
14. National pride
15. Talked himself into a corner
16. One nation, under God, indivisible
17. Face up to reality
18. Half-truths
19. Dual citizenship
20. Rough times
21. Write-off
22. Reversed position
23. A large following
24. The cold war is over at last
25. Right down the middle
26. Open door policy
27. He's involved in politics
28. United States
29. The story is full of holes
30. Inaugural speech

Health Care pgs. 38-42

1. Heart bypass
2. Went into shock
3. Rubdown
4. Emergency
5. Feeling down and out
6. Checks for symptoms
7. Acid indigestion
8. Flat feet
9. A high fever
10. Once-over checkup
11. Counting calories
12. Paramedics
13. Fallen arch
14. Red Cross
15. Broken collarbones
16. Growing older
17. Laid up in the hospital
18. Low-fat diet
19. Doubled over in pain
20. Common cold
21. Coming down with pneumonia
22. Painful back injuries
23. Feeling down in the dumps
24. Bacterial infection
25. Health insurance
26. A sight for sore eyes
27. Hygiene
28. Double-strength aspirin tablets
29. Ankle broken in two places
30. Flat on one's back

Legal pgs. 44-48

1. Double jeopardy
2. Read between the lines
3. Cross examines
4. I am innocent
5. Equal protection under the law
6. Downright devious
7. Ends up behind bars
8. Murder in the first degree
9. Dead to rights
10. I am following your advice
11. Everything's aboveboard now
12. A parting statement
13. Divide it among the heirs
14. Copyright infringement
15. Gross injustice
16. Quick adlibs
17. Don't underrate lawyers
18. Life in prison or capital punishment
19. It's against the law
20. Released from her contract
21. Appearing before a judge
22. Am I under arrest?
23. Mistrial
24. Back up your argument
25. Easy on the wallet
26. A crooked lawyer
27. You are under oath
28. That's beside the point
29. A step ahead of the law
30. A breakthrough in the case

Management pgs. 50-54

1. Staying ahead of the game
2. Down to earth
3. A small fish in a big pond
4. Lonely at the top
5. Domineering
6. Head in the sand
7. Orders from the boss
8. Thinking over the idea
9. Foremost authorities
10. Solving problems together
11. Total quality
12. A breed apart
13. One step forward, two steps back
14. He's above me in salary
15. Keep after him
16. Looking out for number one
17. Big egos
18. Wrapped up in her work
19. She's on top of it
20. Strong tendencies
21. He's high on the plan
22. Am I in charge?
23. He's against everything
24. Sidewalk superintendents
25. Top banana
26. Profitless venture
27. Big cheese
28. Sees about doing it
29. A pat on the back
30. Downright difficult

Manufacturing pgs. 56-60

1. Be on time
2. Rising costs
3. Works around the clock
4. Right down to the wire
5. It's in short supply
6. Backlog
7. A tall order
8. Overstocked warehouse or The warehouse is overstocked
9. Closed down for repairs
10. Made in Taiwan
11. Year-end inventory
12. A little time away from the job
13. Back to the salt mines
14. A prophet without honor
15. A little behind in his work
16. Stayed on a tight schedule
17. A turnover in staff
18. Deadline
19. Shortage
20. A bit behind schedule
21. Outstanding work
22. Back-breaking work
23. Consistency
24. Finished right on time
25. On-time delivery or Delivery on time
26. Part-time jobs
27. Employee turnover
28. Scheduled on alternate Mondays
29. Racing against the clock
30. Across-the-board pay increase or Pay increase across the board

Sports pgs. 62-66

1. Backspin
2. Weightlifting
3. Box seats
4. Bowling
5. Agony of defeat
6. Limber up
7. Three up and three down
8. High ratings
9. A hole in one
10. Won in a big way
11. Tourneys
12. Forfeits
13. Sunday afternoon football
14. Semifinals
15. Ten-speed bicycles
16. Incomplete pass
17. Close calls
18. Caught on the second bounce
19. I am into jogging
20. Season tickets
21. Timeout
22. Too close to call
23. Finished in first place
24. Extra innings
25. Runner-up in the Olympics
26. Corner pocket
27. Lost by a nose
28. The second half of the game
29. Bet on the right horse
30. A slow start and a fast finish

Technical pgs. 68-72

1. Terminal
2. Formats
3. Printout
4. Battery backup
5. Laptop
6. Indexed file
7. Silicon Valley
8. Spread sheet
9. Download
10. Exit
11. Keyboards
12. Vertical scroll bar
13. High density
14. Double click
15. Left justify
16. Semi-conductor
17. Memory upgrade
18. On-line service
19. Tutorials
20. The system is down
21. E-mail
22. Spacebar
23. Text box
24. Turnkey system
25. Hands-on experience
26. Boot up
27. Dot matrix
28. Cursor keys
29. Checks for misspelled words
30. Initialize

Transportation pgs. 74-78

1. Careless driver
2. Airport terminals
3. Standby passengers
4. Departing flights
5. Two weeks overseas
6. Two-car garage
7. Cross country
8. Flies around the country
9. Travel adventure
10. Broken-down cars
11. Blind intersection (No i's)
12. Look both ways before crossing
13. White sidewall tires
14. A half-hour before takeoff
15. High gear
16. Semi driver
17. No U-turn
18. Back up the car
19. Dangerous curves
20. A flat tire
21. Highway overpass
22. Lay over for a few days
23. Engine repairs
24. A long time away from home
25. The plane arrived right on time
26. A fork in the road
27. Flying above the clouds
28. Waits around for hours
29. Car in reverse gear
30. Auto parts

Miscellaneous pgs. 80-89

1. Worlds apart
2. Bend the rules
3. Edgy
4. The center of gravity
5. Small talk
6. Falling behind
7. Choose up sides
8. Compares
9. Day before yesterday
10. I understand
11. It is not inevitable
12. Single-spaced
13. I feel left out
14. A big letdown
15. No end in sight
16. Sit in the corner
17. Angry over nothing
18. The difference between right and wrong
19. The beginning of time
20. An inside joke
21. Turning points
22. Subdivided
23. He follows through
24. Fundraising
25. Wish upon a star
26. Boring
27. Abbreviated version
28. He's under attack
29. A little higher
30. Incomplete sentence

31. Look back
32. High intensity
33. Noteworthiness
34. Different opinions or
    A difference of opinion
35. A meeting of the minds
36. Hair-raising adventure
37. Having it both ways
38. Shadowy
39. Rewritten
40. Nationwide
41. Step down graciously
42. Runs about a mile
43. Growing anxious
44. Capitalistic
45. Holy mackeral
46. Counting sheep
47. Look high and low
48. A second job on the side
49. A turn of events
50. World without end
51. She rose above it
52. Double park
53. A round of applause
54. Eliminate the middle man
55. Clerical error
56. Helplessness
57. A circle of friends
58. Sugar cube
59. Silver quarters
60. The middle of the road